PRESERVING
the
PENNSYLVANIA WILDS

PRESERVING
the
PENNSYLVANIA WILDS

THE REBIRTH OF ELK COUNTRY

Mario L. Chiappelli

*Foreword by Rawland D. Cogan, Cofounder, President
and CEO of the Keystone Elk Country Alliance*

Published by The History Press
Charleston, SC
www.historypress.com

Front cover, top, left to right: Redbellied woodpecker. *Willard Hill, 2020*; Collage art of a Pennsylvania elk by American artist Gina Torkos; Foxes, also an important component of Pennsylvania's ecosystem. *Willard Hill, 2021*; *bottom*: Two elk battling at Bennetts Branch. *David Anderson, 2015*.
Back cover, clockwise from bottom: *Stary Bugle* by American artist David Anderson; Joseph Trimble Rothrock, known for his love of nature and Pennsylvania's forests. *Library of Congress, 1919*; *Battle at the Bennetts Branch* by American artist David Anderson.

First published 2023

Manufactured in the United States

ISBN 9781467155281

Library of Congress Control Number: 2023938569

Notice: The information in this book is true and complete to the best of our knowledge. It is offered without guarantee on the part of the authors or The History Press. The authors and The History Press disclaim all liability in connection with the use of this book.

None of this would have been possible without my family, who have impressed on me the importance of preserving, protecting and continually improving the area that I will always call home—Weedville, Pennsylvania.

CONTENTS

FOREWORD

$\mathcal{E}$lk County, Pennsylvania, named after the easternmost wild elk herd in the United States, and the village of Benezette, located in the Bennetts Valley area known as the "Elk Capital of Pennsylvania," are very familiar to Mario Chiappelli. The author grew up in Pennsylvania's Elk Country and has strong family ties and childhood memories in the Valley. I've known the author's family for many years, his grandfather Donald, grandmother Nancy, dad Bryan, uncle Robbie, his great aunt and uncle Joe and Diane Caliari; been to their camp Buttermilk Lodge; and walked their land. Their home in Weedville is less than half a mile away from my home. The history of Pennsylvania elk is woven in the fiber of this young author, just born in 2000. Therefore, writing this book was the perfect chronicle for Mario because so many of the characters and locations are familiar names and places to him. How appropriate that Mario, an Elk County native, would write *Preserving the Pennsylvania Wilds: The Rebirth of Elk Country*, the most comprehensive account of the history of Pennsylvania's elk.

I moved to Elk County in 1982 and raised a family, worked and still live in this same valley. On September 7, 1982, I began my career working for the Pennsylvania Game Commission researching Pennsylvania's elk herd. During the next twenty years, agency personnel and I studied elk home range and movements, seasonal habitat preferences, recruitment, calf survival, cause and number of known elk mortalities, elk and human conflicts and population survey techniques. After eight years in the field, I entered Penn State University to begin my master's degree program. Shortly afterward, it occurred to me after doing this research that the reason the elk herd was not increasing in numbers was not a biological factor, it was a sociological one: elk had little to no value to people. Once research findings were made available to the public and habitats were improved on the public land base, the herd increased, mostly due to better habitat management, increased public awareness and support.

Preserving the Pennsylvania Wilds is a detailed narrative of the wildlife conservation history of Pennsylvania. The author's many accounts of habitat and wildlife degradation in the Valley is the history of sustainable forestry, the negative effects of market hunting, wildlife habitat degradation and water and air pollution as told through Pennsylvania's elk herd. This book is a historic look at how Pennsylvania's natural resources transformed the state into an industrial machine. There were economic booms and revolutions in the extraction of our natural resources, but these came with a big environmental price tag. Pennsylvania then began the long and arduous road to restoring our state's natural resources and, in the process, began to shape the national conservation movement.

A ROLEX TIMEPIECE IS intricate and complex, with many internal parts like springs, gears, wheels and cogs. When working in unison, it is a marvel of human engineering, but if any one piece is damaged, the watch will not work. Conversely, Mother Nature is not built this way; it is a good thing she is not. Mother Nature can heal, and humanity can learn and help nature heal, which is the reason Pennsylvania is known as the "Cradle of Conservation."

Today, the Keystone Elk Country Alliance manages and operates the Elk Country Visitor Center in Benezette, which attracts 400,000 to 500,000 visitors a year. The alliance provides high-quality elk viewing and educational programs, enhances elk and other wildlife habitat, permanently protects land and drives economic development in the region. Conserving and enhancing Pennsylvania's Elk Country for future generations is good, but building a world-class destination that creates jobs and an economic engine for the region that will continue to conserve and enhance Pennsylvania's Elk Country is even better.

The author, much wiser than his years, completely understands the importance of conserving our natural resources and the intrinsic value wildlife provides in our everyday life. His accounts of the past remind us of where we have been, the mistakes we have made, the sociological transformation of the importance of our natural resources and that the future is bright for Pennsylvania's elk herd. Today, the elk herd in Pennsylvania is thriving, providing viewing and hunting opportunities, creating jobs and fueling economic development within the region—the definition of a wildlife success story.

In fact, the author has included throughout *Preserving the Pennsylvania Wilds* the historical accounts that led to the greatest wildlife conservation story ever told; this is the story of the North American Model of Wildlife Conservation, the world's most successful system of policies and laws to restore and safeguard fish and wildlife and their habitats through sound science and active management.

—Rawland Cogan, wildlife biologist
President and CEO of Keystone Elk Country Alliance (KECA)

PREFACE

With a year left in college, through the consultation of my academic advisors and multiple department chairs, I made the decision to pursue a double major in history in conjunction with my degree in computer engineering. After sacrificing all of my elective space and taking summer classes, as of May 2, 2022, I had officially completed the necessary course requirements to complete a degree in history from Bucknell University.

The last requirement of the degree was to complete HIST 400, a class designed for students to engage in a research topic of their choosing and to formulate an analytical research paper. This is the culminating experience that the History Department at Bucknell University offers its students.

I chose to research a topic that is important to me, my family and the community that I grew up in. I decided to tell the history of Pennsylvania's elk herd, with specific attention being paid toward the industrial practices that played direct roles in limiting the survival of the elk and how it took centuries of poor conservation practices to convince Pennsylvanians that something needed to be done to preserve the natural beauty and wildlife of the state. This book evolved from my original thirty-page essay from that class because I felt a need to tell the story in its entirety and expose the journey and hardships that the elk faced. As it stands, there is a lack of scholarship that engages the full scope history of Pennsylvania's elk herd, and my hope is that this work starts to fill that void.

Preserving the Pennsylvania Wilds closely examines primary source materials throughout the eighteenth, nineteenth, twentieth and twenty-first centuries, which are then brought together to form the story of Pennsylvania's conservation journey. While containing sizable chunks of source material, this narrative was crafted in a way that is intended to give readers an opportunity to examine the primary materials for themselves in tandem with my analysis.

ACKNOWLEDGEMENTS

J would like to personally thank my history teachers for helping me pursue a degree in history, specifically Professors Claire Campbell, John Enyeart and David Del Testa. My editor, Tabitha Chilton, deserves a major thank-you, not only for spending countless hours combing through the many iterations of this book but also for giving keen insight on areas to hone in on and expand. In addition, I want to thank Rawland Cogan of the Keystone Elk Country Alliance for writing the foreword and being a great authoritative resource for the development of this book.

Additionally, I want to thank Jim Burke and the Mt. Zion Historical Society for being a great resource for historical images and proofreading. Also Marcia and Don Bleggi of the St. Marys Historical Society deserve my gratitude for directly assisting me in my research process.

A very special thank-you is in order for my aunt Gina Torkos for providing the artwork for the cover of the book. Also, I greatly appreciate all of the local photographers who allowed me to use their images and artwork throughout this book, specifically Ronald J. Saffer, David Anderson, Willard Hill, Bob Traveny and Tom Dorsey. David Anderson also provided a great collection of personal artwork that is integrated throughout *Preserving the Pennsylvania Wilds*.

INTRODUCTION

S trapped into a car seat in the back of my father's Toyota Tacoma, we left our home in Force, Pennsylvania. We were on our way to our hunting camp. Known as the Buttermilk Lodge, it is located on top of Rock Hill in between the towns of Medix Run and Caledonia. Before making any serious headway, we needed to stop at the local gas station and convenience store, the Valley Farm Market, to refuel on gas and to buy a few sticks of pepperoni to snack on throughout the day. We then picked up a family friend, Eddie Zuchelli.

We were heading to camp not for the typical squirrel, deer or even turkey hunt but for something more unique: today was the first day of elk hunting season. The year before, in 2001, the Pennsylvania Game Commission officially reinstated the famed hunt. Seventy years prior, 1931, was the last time anyone could legally hunt elk in Pennsylvania, and here I was, in the second year of its reintroduction, about to participate in a great Pennsylvania elk hunt.

As a two-year-old, my roles and responsibilities were limited to helping my dad and Eddie extract elk as well as serve as an audible alarm clock for when meals needed to take place. Other, more experienced hunters were guides for those who were lucky enough to have received an elk tag. Many of my family members had become registered elk hunting guides with the Pennsylvania Game Commission. Under the leadership of my grandfather Donald Chiappelli and Zio (Italian for uncle) Robbie Chiappelli, the elk

Rock Hill Outdoor Adventures hunting guides loading a bull elk into a truck. *Arthur Martin, 2021.*

guiding service Rock Hill Outdoor Adventures was formed and has since guided ambitious hunters for over twenty years in Jay and Benezette Townships.

Since the hunting season was open for one week out of the year and I was attending school, the amount of time I could spend participating was inherently limited. However, one day after coming home from middle school, as I was walking down my driveway, I noticed my Zio Robbie's truck approaching from behind. He briefly stopped and told me to hop in the bed because one of the hunters shot an elk about a mile behind my house. When we arrived at the scene, I saw that it was a beautiful bull elk, one of the largest I had ever seen. I watched Zio Robbie field dress the animal, and when he was done, I helped lift the bull into my father's side-by-side so it could be extracted from the woods and eventually taken to the elk check station.

The word *elk* comes from the German *elch*, the name for the European moose. Elk are the second-largest member of the deer family, surpassed only by the moose. A mature bull elk stands nearly sixty inches at the shoulder and weighs up to one thousand pounds; females, or cows, can weigh up to six hundred pounds. Elk are herbivores and tend to eat grasses, oats and various foliage.

Elk are not native to North America. They originated in Asia and eventually migrated across the Bering Strait, a landmass that once connected modern-day Siberia and Alaska. Elk were one of the many species of game that Native Americans pursued into North America during the Ice Age. A subspecies of elk that closely resembles their American counterpart is prevalent throughout Mongolia.[1]

While I may not have always had a hands-on role during the elk season, my grandfather still put me to work. In order to participate in an elk hunt, a pool of people is randomly drawn and awarded tags. In recent years, the drawing has been held at the Elk Country Visitor Center on top of Winslow Hill, near Benezette, during the yearly Elk Expo, and has become a massive community event. As hunters are selected, some identifying information of each person is displayed on a big screen in the visitor center's outdoor classroom area. The Pennsylvania Game Commission stopped publishing each hunter's full information, so the only way to ascertain a list of hunters was to write down their names in a mad scramble as they were announced. To make it even harder, the only data that was presented to the public was the hunter's first initial, last name and town of residence. Since no contact information is provided, I was tasked with researching each individual hunter in the hopes of finding either their phone number or email address

Swiss artist Peter Rindisbacher's painting titled *European Elk*. *John Davis Hatch Collection.*

in order to contact them and advertise my grandfather's guiding service. As years passed, this job became easier, due to a greater amount of people spending time online. When I finally convinced my grandfather to purchase a Whitepages subscription, the identification process became trivial.

Acquiring an elk license in Pennsylvania has become akin to winning the lottery. In 2020, first-time hunters had a 1 in 9,173 chance (approximately 0.0109 percent) to draw a bull elk tag.[2] Hunters from all across the state and the country pay and apply just to have a slight chance to receive a tag. In 2022, the cost to purchase one of these chances was $11.95.

Pennsylvania elk hunting was wildly popular during its return in 2001, when over fifty thousand people applied and only thirty permits were awarded.[3] Those that do not want to play a game of chance have an opportunity to win the Governor's Tag. Since 2009, affluent hunters could bid on the opportunity to receive a guaranteed elk license. In its first year, the tag sold for $28,000, and in 2022 the winning bid was approximately $275,000.[4] Those who purchased the Governor's Tag truly believed they were receiving a once-in-a-lifetime opportunity. Considering that elk can be more easily hunted at a much cheaper rate in the western parts of the United States, there had to be something truly unique about a Pennsylvania elk hunting experience.

Pennsylvania's elk have long been viewed as a natural and immensely popular spectacle since early in the state's history. Famed outdoorsman Philip Tome was an avid hunter in the north-central region of Pennsylvania during the late eighteenth and early nineteenth centuries. In 1854, he wrote a book on his many wildlife experiences in the region. *Pioneer Life, or 30 Years a Hunter* captured the true essence of a hunter's life in Pennsylvania's wilderness through accounts of the region's terrain; descriptions of common animal habits; and stories of hunting bears, panthers and deer. Though by far the biggest subject matter was how Tome hunted elk. Throughout, Tome continually described them as being "noble" creatures and in one account stated that

> *the elk is the lord of the forest in which he ranges, no animal inhabiting the same localities being able to conquer him. Terrific combats sometimes ensue amongst themselves, and I have often found them dead in the woods, with deep wounds made by the antlers of their antagonists.*[5]

In the same manner that the lion is considered the king of the jungle, Tome adamantly believed that the elk were among the ruling class of Pennsylvania's forests.

What are perhaps the most fascinating accounts that Tome provided are his adventures in capturing live, full-grown elk. In the winter of 1816–17,

Early 1900s painting of a European elk fighting wolves. *Julian Falat.*

Tome described how he and a companion of his, a Mr. Campbell, successfully captured what Tome claimed to be the largest elk he had ever seen.

> *I let the dogs go, they attacked him vigorously, and he ran south ten miles to Kettle Creek. He then ran around a hill, and turned up the east branch which he ascended four miles on the ice, when he broke through, into the water about four feet deep. Here the dogs worried him, as we judged, about two hours, when he started again, ran up a hill, and halted on a rock. The dogs pursued him to the rock, and then returned to us. We met them two or three miles from the elk, which had taken a circuitous course, so that the track at one place was but a fourth of a mile from the rock on which he was stationed, while it was two miles to follow the track. The dogs tried to go directly to the elk, but we thought they saw something else, and compelled them to keep the track, reaching the elk about dark. Campbell made ready the rope, while I cut a pole about 15 feet long. He went to the south side of the rock with the dogs, to call his attention in that direction, while I mounted the rock on the north side, and endeavored to put the rope over his horns with the pole. He wheeled and came toward me, when I jumped from the rock, and he turned again to the dogs. About eight feet from the rock stood a hemlock tree, about two feet in diameter, with branches six or eight feet above the ground. It occurred to me that if I could climb this it would be an easy matter to slip the noose over the horns of the elk. I made the attempt, but did not succeed as my moccasins were frozen. I pulled them off and tried again, but with no better success. I then took off my coat, which was by no means pleasant, as the weather was intensely cold, but it enabled me to climb the tree. Campbell then passed the pole and rope up to me, and called off the dogs. I shouted, and the elk turned and advanced toward me, when I slipped the noose over his horns, and with a jerk drew it tight. I then descended and attached the end of the rope to a tree about forty feet from the elk, and we pulled him from the rock.*[6]

Tome and Campbell eventually brought the elk back to Coudersport, where the animal was appraised to be worth $1,000 (about $20,500 today). Before selling the elk, Tome took it on a tour throughout the neighboring towns, among them Olean, New York. He put the large bull on exhibit and charged those who wished to see it. Even people from the most rural regions, who lived among elk, paid top dollar to see Tome's proudest capture. Viewing elk became a spectacle that still exists today, and Tome knew how to take full advantage of it.

Drawing from *Wild Life in the Far West* by James Hobbes. *1874.*

After capturing nearly a dozen live elk, Tome eventually gave up the practice due to the tremendous risks and decreasing profitability. Hunting elk primarily took place during the winter months because it made tracking the animals incredibly easier. Throughout Tome's accounts, he and his companions would traverse many miles of mountainous terrain in freezing temperatures, miles from any form of civilization. The last elk that Tome captured alive was sold for just over $100. While he does not provide any reason for the decrease in value, one can assume that having domesticated elk was a luxury not many could afford.

Aside from procuring a profit, Tome also believed that elk would make valuable livestock if enough were able to be placated.

> *A female elk will stand and suffer herself to be milked, and their milk is nearly equal to that of a cow, both in quality and quantity. In my opinion the elk would prove a valuable addition to our stock of domestic animals, if introduced among them. It possesses strength and speed superior to any other cloven-footed animal, while for food or milk they are equally valuable, their growth is very rapid, and they are easily kept in good condition. Indeed, all the qualities which render the reindeer so indispensable to the inhabitants of Lapland, are possessed by the elk.[7]*

In the eyes of Tome, the elk were the quintessential animal. They were the animal kingdom's equivalent of Leonardo da Vinci's Vitruvian Man—a creature possessing every desirable characteristic imaginable. Tome even claimed that the only animal that could successfully face off against a bear and win was a bull elk. It should be noted that Tome never witnessed the two species square off but instead purported it via his expertise as an outdoorsman and hunter.[8]

Perhaps Tome was not alone in believing that elk were near perfect animals of a more noble species. Known for his macabre horror style of poetry, Edgar Allan Poe was also an admirer of Pennsylvania's elk. Considered one of Pennsylvania's earliest nature writers and enthusiasts, Poe documented an encounter with an elk while observing nature along the Wissahickon River near Philadelphia in 1844:

What I saw upon this cliff, although surely an object of very extraordinary nature, the place and season considered, at first neither startled nor amazed me—so thoroughly and appropriately did it chime in with the half-slumberous fancies that enwrapped me. I saw, or dreamed that I saw, standing upon the extreme verge of the precipice, with neck outstretched, with ears erect, and the whole attitude indicative of profound and melancholy inquisitive, one of the oldest and boldest of those identical elks which had been coupled with the red men of my vision.

I say that, for a few moments, this apparition neither startled nor amazed me. During this interval my whole soul was bound up in intense sympathy alone. I fancied the elk repining, not less than wondering, at the manifest alterations for the worse, wrought upon the brook and its vicinage, even within the last few years, by the stern hand of the utilitarian. But a slight movement of the animal's head at once dispelled the dreaminess which invested me, and aroused me to a full sense of the novelty of the adventure. I arose upon one knee within the skiff, and, while I hesitated whether to stop my career, or let myself float nearer to the object of my wonder, I heard the words "hist! hist!" ejaculated quickly but cautiously, from the shrubbery overhead. In an instant afterwards, a negro emerged from the thicket, putting aside the bushes with care, and treading stealthily. He bore in one hand a quantity of salt, and, holding it towards the elk, gently yet steadily approached. The noble animal, although a little fluttered, made no attempt at escape. The negro advanced; offered the salt; and spoke a few words of encouragement or conciliation. Presently, the elk bowed and stamped, and then lay quietly down and was secured with a halter.

Stereoscopic view of an elk in Yellowstone Park from the early nineteenth century. The caption calls it the "Lordly Monarch of Western Wilds." *Keystone View Company.*

> *Thus ended my romance of the elk. It was a pet of great age and very domestic habits, and belonged to an English family occupying a villa in the vicinity.*[9]

While Poe was dismayed to see that the elk was tamed, that does not discount the paralysis of awe that "bound up his soul." Unfortunately for the famed poet, he was one of the last people to see elk in Pennsylvania; within twenty years, the last of the elk had vanished from the state.

Pennsylvania's elk became extinct, and thus the mythology and lore surrounding the animal was allowed to propagate. Elk were viewed in a sacrosanct manner that continued well throughout Pennsylvania's history. Eventually, the species was reintroduced, and those that lived in proximity to the elk viewed them as members of their community. In the 1980s, the Pennsylvania Game Commission announced that plans for a new elk hunting season were in the works. Many were excited, but those who resided near the herd were furious. According to Joe Kosack, an information specialist with the Pennsylvania Game Commission, many of the local people were upset that out-of-towners were going to kill "their elk."[10] The herd at this time was small, hovering around a population of one hundred, and many did not want to see this species become extinct in Pennsylvania again.

My whole life I have been surrounded by the elk. It is common to see them in massive herds or small pairings traveling in my neighborhood. Oftentimes, I can peer out my window and see them resting in my backyard. My dog has a strong tendency to greet them with a violent onslaught of barking and growling. However, Jake, a twenty-five-pound cockapoo, does little to actually intimidate the elk. As Jake sprints around and underneath the elk, they do nothing more than give him a confused glare.

As evidenced by Jake's wildly ineffective defense antics, elk can be incredibly approachable animals. One evening, I was driving my side-by-side along my grandfather's hunting property on Rock Hill. I came into a clearing where

Photo of a bull elk taken near homes in Force, Pennsylvania. *Bob Traveny, 2020.*

I saw a lone cow elk. It was a young animal, no more than two years old. Knowing how passive elk are, I thought it would be worth an attempt to see how close I could get without spooking it. Eventually, I got within a range of ten feet, stopped and decided that was enough encroachment. The young elk stared at me, and I stared back. I spent the next few minutes pondering how amazingly unique it was to be able to stand this close to a wild animal that doubled me in size, without an inkling of fear. When it was time to leave, I gave the elk a slight nod and departed.

The elk bugle is a sound that cannot be unheard. It is an excitement that gives me goosebumps still to this day. An elk's bugle is a wavering pitch between high and low tones combined in unison to form a perfect harmony. No words can accurately describe the sound because it is just that unique. Even so, many who witness the elk bugle try to ascribe words to it. Ed Wetschler of the *New York Times* offered his own account during a 2005 trip to Benezette:

> *The shriek started off like the creak of a rusty hinge and shifted to a cross between a whistle and a screaming jazz horn—with the volume set on 11. A group of fat wild turkeys hurried into the air, scared skyward. I almost levitated, too. It was the sound we had been waiting for, the storied bugling of a male elk.*[11]

Wetschler was lucky enough to experience this on his trip to the region. The emotions and excitement that he felt are the same that I feel, still, every time I hear the ceremonious bugle.

While obtaining an elk license is incredibly unlikely, residents have the opportunity to extract a trophy from these animals without having to go on any form of traditional hunt. Every spring, the elk, along with deer, shed their antlers throughout the forests, and these deposed antlers prove to be widely sought after. Many people train dogs to sniff out the antlers, while others simply scour the woods in teams.

In the spring of 2021, a large bull elk had been seen walking through my backyard on multiple occasions. Both my father and I knew that it was only a matter of time until the animal shed its antlers, leaving them for the public domain. Then one afternoon, my dad noticed that the same elk returned with no antlers at all. We immediately set out in search of the two fallen trophies in the woods directly behind our house. Within a few minutes, we found one of the antlers. Its counterpart was not found until about an hour later, located approximately one mile from where we started. Being able to find one elk shed is rare, but finding a matching set is a dream come true.

Pennsylvania's elk are truly special creatures. They are the living icon of the small region in north-central Pennsylvania that I call home. The elk are members of my community, and as many people travel here to observe the elk, they, too, experience the immense awe and excitement that I feel nearly every day.

The natural landscape of this region was reshaped over the course of the last three centuries, and with it many species came and left. By the end of the 1860s, the last native elk had been killed in Pennsylvania, and that is where this story begins.

1

WHERE'D ALL THE WILD THINGS GO?

*O*n October 21, 1888, the *New York Times* published an article titled "The Last of the Wapiti: A Forty-Mile Chase After a Lone Elk." The word *wapiti*, meaning "white rump," is the term that the Shawnee and Cree used to describe the enormous and magnificent elk. The piece gave an account of how Jim Jacobs, a resident of a Seneca reservation in New York, led a two-day hunt in pursuit of what was largely believed to be the last living elk in north-central Pennsylvania. At the age of seventy-five, Jacobs, with the help of another Native American and his pack of hunting dogs, traversed rough mountainous terrain in the harsh November snow in search of the elk. Eventually, the crew of hunters came upon the elk on the Clarion River some forty miles from their original location. According to the *New York Times*, the last of the Pennsylvania wapitis' fate was described in this account:

> *The animal baffled pursuit for days, but the Indian hunters were as tireless as their game, and on the fourth day, after starting the elk, two of them through a heavy snowstorm, the game was brought to bay in the forests of Clarion County, near the headwaters of the Clarion River, 40 miles from the point where the trail was first struck, although twice that distance, if not more, had been covered in the chase. When the two Indians arrived on the spot where the elk had been forced to turn on its pursuers, they found it surrounded by the dogs and fiercely fighting them. Jim Jacobs was anxious to secure the noble animal alive, and hours were spent by the two Indians*

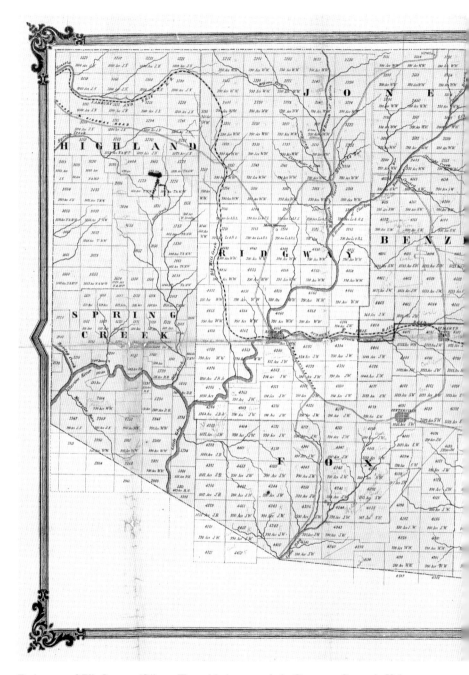

Early map of Elk County (Gibson Township is presently in Cameron County). *H.A. Pattison, 1855.*

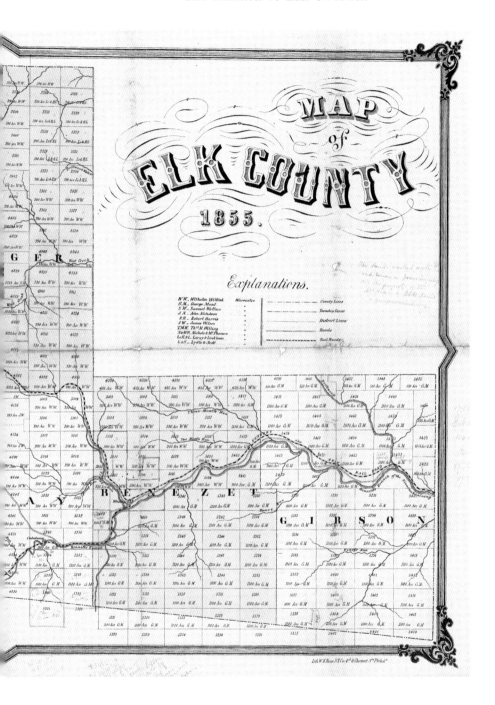

in efforts to that end, but they were useless. Jim Jacobs shot it through the heart, and the last of the wapiti race in Pennsylvania—the "lone elk of the Sinnemahoning"—died defying its enemies to the end.[12]

Samuel A. King, a professor of history at the Pennsylvania State University of DuBois, recognized the legitimacy of Jacobs's story in a detailed map titled *Lore of the Last Frontier in Pennsylvania* that was published by the Clearfield County Historical Society in 1960. In a small excerpt, King credits Jacobs with killing the last elk. He even goes as far as to reaffirm the notion that the last bull was indeed a resilient fighter that died defying Jacobs and his partner by claiming that the "old bull was too tough to eat." One inconsistency occurred in his brief account in that he stated that Jacobs's famed hunt took place in 1864, while the *New York Times* article claimed it took place three years after, in 1867.[13]

This discrepancy, along with other stories of Jacobs that offer differing claims, have resulted in the famed hunt being received as nothing more than lore of the north-central Pennsylvania region. Regardless of the timeline's accuracy, what is certain is that the majestic elk of Pennsylvania were extinct. Elk County received its name because it was the site of Pennsylvania's last surviving elk herd, and twenty years after its founding, the state's last elk had been killed.

While elk still remained in the western reaches of the United States, they were now entirely gone from Pennsylvania. Although later elk reintroduction efforts were attempted due to the federal government's program to reduce rapidly growing herds at Yellowstone National Park, unnatural and reckless environmental practices inhibited any possibility of sustainability in Pennsylvania. Overhunting in tandem with the lumber and mining industries severely altered the natural landscape and became seemingly immovable barriers in the way of having a thriving elk herd. Eventually, however, through many state institutions and the willpower of centuries of Pennsylvania conservationists, the elk population would have a chance to prosper once again.

One of the main regions in which the last elk herd lived and where the modern herd primarily resides is known as Bennetts Valley. The Valley, as it is more commonly referred to, is a small conglomeration of towns that are inherently defined by their ruralness and natural wildlife. These towns include Weedville, Force, Byrnedale, Hollywood, Tyler, Caledonia, Medix Run, Grant, Dents Run and Benezette, most of which fall under Jay or Benezette Township in southeastern Elk County. The biggest of these towns are Byrnedale and Weedville, which boast a population of 500 and 465, respectively. Force is the only other town mentioned that has a designated census status, with a population of 166. The entirety of Benezette Township, which includes Medix Run, Grant, Dents Run and Benezette, has a population of 207. All of the population data came from 2018 census projections.[14] These towns are unquestionably small, and their significance in history should be rightfully questioned. However, this community eventually became home to the largest elk herd in the northeastern United States. It will take learning from the mistakes of nearly two centuries of environmental abuse to finally right the wrongs of the past, the first of which is overhunting, an addiction that became unmanageable and detrimental for all of Pennsylvania's wildlife.

Although Jacobs, who hunted up until he was ninety years old, was considered by the aforementioned *New York Times* article "the greatest hunter that ever roamed the woods of that country" and had presumably harvested many other game prior, he should not be blamed for his participation in his legendary hunt. Instead, blame should fall on the culture of overhunting that was extremely common throughout America's early history. In the same *New York Times* article that described Jacobs's hunt, the author recalled a man named Seth Nelson who allegedly had records of killing thirty-seven elk between the years 1830 and 1843. The author claimed to have met with Nelson in his home near what is now Round Island, Cameron County, in 1883.[15]

It is important to recognize that Nelson and Jacobs were not alone as far as perpetrators of unethical conservation practices were concerned. In fact, there are many romanticized accounts of elk hunts that took place prior to their extinction. In a Sunday edition of the *Philadelphia Times* in 1894, an unnamed correspondent recalled a time in which he embarked on an elk hunt with the locally renowned hunters Jack and Laroy Lyman in Potter County during the fall of 1864. The Lyman brothers offered to take the author to a location where they knew about four or five elk commonly resided. In response, the author asked, "Why not get them all?" This comment was simply brushed off by Laroy Lyman, who smugly responded, "One will be enough." It was clear that the author did not have an appreciation for conservation, and his actions would soon prove it. Only fifteen minutes after shooting his prized elk, he fired at a large buck. The Lyman brothers were not pleased with the actions of the author; in fact, they were irate. After being severely admonished by Jack Lyman, the author said, "I wanted a panther to come out of the woods and do me the favor to chew me up, I felt so downright sneaking."[16]

The author clearly did not share the same level of appreciation for Pennsylvania's wildlife as the Lyman brothers. As indicated by his reaction, he was surprised that what he did was considered wrong. Convincing one-time hunters and others that the wild game of Pennsylvania needed to be conserved would be one of the toughest battles for early conservationists.

Poor hunting practices were not limited to the north-central region of Pennsylvania. In a book written by Randolph Keim titled *Sheridan's Troopers on the Border*, he recounted his journey with Lieutenant General Phil Sheridan, who, in 1868, led an expedition throughout the southern plains of North America in order to quell Native American uprisings. Toward the end of their campaign, Keim and Sheridan employed a local Native American as a guide for an elk hunt.

After taking shots at and presumably wounding multiple elk and deer, Keim wrote, "the General and I were wandering about without any very definite ideas of what we were hunting, but acting under the general principle of taking a shot at everything that came within range."[17] In saying this, Keim publicly admitted that overhunting was a common practice. In fact, the sheer notion of two high-ranking army officers engaging in this behavior lends a certain credibility and prestige to that practice.

Philip Tome, who hunted the north-central region of Pennsylvania for over thirty years, was vehemently against the wanton destruction of any animal. He believed that it was the hunter's basic duty to respect the natural landscape and not extract anything that proved to be of no value. Tome used this theme when he described his opinion on the prestige of hunting and how to not allow the excitement of the hunt to corrupt one's motives:

> With a true hunter it is not the destruction of life which affords the pleasure of the chase; it is the excitement attendant upon the very uncertainty of it which induces men even to leave luxurious homes and expose themselves to the hardships and perils of the wilderness. Even when, after a weary chase, the game is brought down, he cannot, after the first thrill of triumph, look without a pang of remorse, upon the form which was so beautifully adapted to its situation, and which his hand has reduced to a mere lump of flesh. But with us, who made our homes in the wilderness, there was a stronger motive than love of excitement for seeking out and destroying the denizens of the forest. We did it in obedience to the primal law of nature: for subsistance or defence of ourselves and those whom we were bound by the ties of nature to support and defend. When neither of these demanded the destruction of an animal, I never felt any desire to harm it.[18]

Running a Bank of Elk by American artist Alfred Jacob Miller, depicting a scene of two hunters in the Platte Canyon in Colorado. *1837.*

Like Sheridan and the *Philadelphia Times* correspondent, Tome simultaneously explained the attractive force that lured men into the daunting wilderness. He also established the only appropriate justifications for the killing of wild animals. However, the rationale employed by the aforementioned hunters did not align with Tome's justifications of subsistence or self-defense; instead, they sought a purely thrill-seeking adventure.

While Tome had a clear standard for practicing ethical hunting, his definition of subsistence does not correlate well to a modern understanding. Today, hunters are limited to harvesting game in accordance with bag limits as well as other game laws. In general, as far as big game is concerned, the average hunter cannot harvest more than one animal of a specific species. Tome was not subject to such regulations. He lived during the early nineteenth century in an incredibly rural region that lacked a significant connection to commerce from urbanized areas. The need to hunt to simply provide food for his family forced him to harvest much wild game. In Tome's book, he provided a quantitative description of what he and his brother would typically bring in from a year's worth of hunting.

> *My brother killed from twenty-five to thirty elk and twenty to twenty-five bears each year. I did not kill as many. I usually killed from ten to twenty*

bears, and one season I killed thirty-five elk. By fire-hunting, hunting in the woods, and by hounding deer, my brother has taken as many as seventy in a season....I killed, in one season, from the time we first began to fire-hunt, in June, until the middle of January, forty-seven deer. During one season, my brother killed, of bears, elk and deer, nearly two hundred. The greatest number that I killed, in any one season, of the same kind of animals, was about one hundred and thirty.[19]

It is important to note that Tome did not believe the immense quantity of wild game that he harvested was an overzealous amount. Many of his expeditions, especially elk and bear hunts, required teams of three to six people. These fellow hunters also had families that relied on venison to survive. While the mass killing of these animals can be justified in the name of survival, it is clear that this practice is not sustainable. It should be no surprise that after centuries of these hunting practices, wildlife populations became severely endangered or extinct.

Elk were not the only species that suffered from overhunting during the mid- to late 1800s in Pennsylvania. Large predators, such as timber wolves, panthers and mountain lions, became nearly extinct by the beginning of the twentieth century. This was largely due to bounties issued by the state government. Mountain lion bounties first surfaced in 1802, where adults could fetch a price of $8 (a modern-day value of just over $200).[20] The white-tailed deer population had been severely threatened by the increased demand for venison in conjunction with sustenance hunting practices.

Mainly due to the destruction of its habitat and an immensely profitable market, the passenger pigeon disappeared from the state as well. Abraham R. Beck of Lititz provided a vivid description of a flock that flew over his town in 1846 that indicated how numerous they once were: "The dense mass of pigeons extended overhead seemingly—beheld in perspective—to the eastern horizon, and as far north and south as the eye could reach; and was continuous from about 12:30 to 4:30 p.m."[21]

As the passenger pigeon population began to dwindle, a bird protection movement started to spread in the United States. Some concerned residents of Ohio petitioned their state legislators to protect the wild pigeons. They were met with this response by a senate panel:

The passenger pigeon needs no protection. Wonderfully prolific, having the vast forests of the North as its breeding grounds, traveling hundreds of miles in search of food, it is here today and elsewhere tomorrow, and

Passenger pigeon flock being hunted in Louisiana. *Smith Bennett, 1875.*

no ordinary destruction can lessen them, or be missed from the myriads that are yearly produced.[22]

Unfortunately, this train of thought plagued many people throughout the United States. It was, in their minds, unfathomable to conceive that the abundant wildlife throughout the country could be brought to extinction. This harmful ideology facilitated the extinction of the passenger pigeon, elk and many other species native to Pennsylvania.

In his book *The White-Tailed Deer*, John Madson gave some insight into why so many species were being overhunted in early America. In explaining the impact that the white-tailed deer had on early American society, he claimed:

America grew up eating venison and wearing buckskin. We were weaned as a nation on deer meat, took our first toddling steps in deer hide moccasins, and came of age at King's Mountain and New Orleans when our deer-trained riflemen cut down foreign regulars in long scarlet swaths. We scraped, oiled, and stretched buckskin over our cabin windows in lieu of glass. When the crops were put by, maybe we walked down the mountain to a turnpike or tavern and swapped deer hides for the venomous rum we called "The Crowns Revenge." In early Kaintuck when there was no flour we gave our babies boiled venison instead of bread. Moving west, we spliced the first telegraph lines with buckskin thongs and tipped our 30-foot bullwhips with buckskin poppers. We dressed our heroes in buckskin, gloves and mukluks, and sent them off to Lundy's Lane, the Alamo, the Little Big Horn, Attu, and Aachen. And we're still people of the deer. A pair of wealthy Detroit executives, lunching at their club, grin like boys as they plan the fall deer hunt. A Carolina mountain farmer, waking to find frost in the laurel thickets, oils the lock of his ten-pound "hawg-rifle" and winks at his son.…Anyone from the outcountry knows that a proper man looks first to his Bible, then to his buck rifle, and then to the business of deer. These things done, has put himself in proper order to look after his nation.[23]

Based on his description, Madson contended that America had become addicted to using every aspect of the white-tailed deer. If you asked him what the national symbol of America was, his answer surely would have been a white-tailed deer and not the bald eagle—the white-tailed deer was the identity of the American spirit. This passage from Madson was written in 1961, during a time when deer hunting enthusiasm had reached an all-time high—especially in Pennsylvania, where deer populations had reached exceedingly high levels. Perhaps Madson's claims about deer culture during the nineteenth century were nostalgic recollections biased by his contemporary lens. Nevertheless, there is an immense amount of truth within the notion that many people heavily relied on the deer for subsistence, clothing and other necessities. An overreliance on game was one of the main factors prohibiting early Americans from practicing sustainable hunting methods.

In his book on the history of America's white-tailed deer, Madson chronicled overhunting practices throughout every nook and cranny of the country. After speaking to the effects of market hunting, Madson juxtaposed overhunting's negative outcomes:

The drain to the market was bad enough, but it couldn't compare with the relentless hunting by countless settlers and backwoodsmen who depended on venison as a staple meat.…During the "Massacre Winter" of 1856–57, Iowa settlers butchered the last of their deer and elk in the winter yards, catching the animals in crusted snow and slaughtering them with knives and axes. Georgia backwoodsmen with large packs of fine hounds wiped out their deer in the mountain coves, and the mountaineers in the Great Smokies farther

Study for Rail Shooting from a Punt by Thomas Eakins, showing a hunter firing from a small boat along the Delaware River. *1874.*

> *north set iron deer traps in trails. Southern slaves devised ingenious knife traps for deer runways, and northwoodsmen cruised lakes and rivers at night in canoes, jacklighting deer with torches and panfuls of glowing coals. One old New York trapper who died in 1850 left a lifetime record kill of 2,550 deer.*[24]

The nineteenth century witnessed the innovation of many hunting practices that are now outlawed. When subsistence was the prevailing motive of hunters, any methods necessary to harvest game were employed. Jacklighting, fire-hunting, hunting above salt licks and hunting with dogs were all common practices. Tome actively engaged in all four of these tactics, which, as previously stated, yielded him copious amounts of game. Tome described an account of jacklighting when he was fishing and noticed deer along the banks of the stream. Everyone he was with got into a canoe, and

> *one held the light, another sat in the forward part of the canoe, generally with two guns, and the third one sitting in the stern, would push the canoe upstream as carefully as possible. Sometimes we could approach so near as to shoot them as they raised their heads erect to look at the light. Sometimes they would stand still long enough for the hunter to bring down a second one with the other gun.*[25]

American Hunting Scenes: A Good Chance by Arthur Fitzwilliam Tait, showing hunters in Michigan firing from a small boat. *1863.*

The light that Tome and his fellow hunters shone on the deer transfixed the animal, essentially hypnotizing them for a few seconds, leaving them paralyzed with curiosity and making them temporarily unaware of their surroundings.

In an example of hunting over a salt lick, Tome artificially created one of these baiting devices. Elk and deer were deeply attracted to these fixtures. Tome then climbed a nearby tree or, if none were available, constructed a scaffold, and simply waited, perched in the sky, for some game to become infatuated with the salt lick. It should be of no surprise that both of these practices were soon outlawed by the State of Pennsylvania. It was believed that they exploited deer's weaknesses via manipulation of the senses. However, Tome was not wrong to engage in these strategies; in fact, they were legal and widely practiced. Due to dwindling elk and deer populations, these tactics were outlawed in an effort to protect what was left.

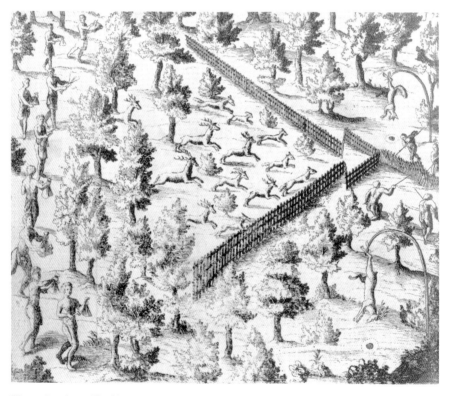

Illustration from *The Observations of Samuel de Champlain* as he traveled North America studying the Native tribes. The heading above the illustration is titled *Indians of North America—Subsistence Activities. 1613.*

The ethics surrounding overhunting also stem from the many financial incentives associated with early wildlife practices. The high demand for various pelts from America's plentiful wildlife populations created a profitable fur economy, and subsequently, many hunters were able to rationalize overhunting as a relative good for themselves and the rest of America.

Many state-sponsored financial incentives to hunt various animals were offered in Pennsylvania throughout its history. William Penn, Pennsylvania's founder, offered bounties for wolves in 1683.[26] Individual counties offered various rates for predatory animal's scalps throughout the early 1800s.[27] Tome benefited mightily from the fur economy and bounties. He once described the monetary gains made from one of his hunting expeditions in the following manner:

> The receipts were forty sable-skins and fifteen deer-skins at seventy-five cents each; the panther's head brought a bounty of six dollars, in all forty-seven dollars and forty-five cents; which, with the venison, was all we obtained.[28]

Tome and other hunters could justifiably sell skins and leftover meat because it was for the benefit of themselves and their families. None of the game they harvested from their hunting practices went to waste.

In 1883, Pennsylvania passed the Scalp Act, which paid out bounties for various scalps from all sorts of predatory animals. A decade later, the *Lancaster Intelligencer* published an article that detailed the corruption and manipulation that was inherent within the legislation:

> We need only recall the absurdities of the Scalp Act of 1883, under which thousands of dollars were paid for bogus wolf and fox scalps, made from the fur of the peaceful mule, and other thousands were squandered on the heads of chickens which were somehow made to pass for piratical owls and hawks in the judgment of intelligent squires. It is even said that owls and hawks were extensively hatched for the bounty.[29]

The article was published just after citizens belonging to the State Sportsmen's Association in Harrisburg lobbied heavily for the creation of a game commission in Pennsylvania. Additionally, the article highlighted how the financial incentives offered by the state resulted in many cheating the system to leech whatever money they could. The law was initially enacted to limit the population of certain predatory species that were growing in numbers. As the rest of the state was in the process of being settled, bounties were considered necessary to protect Pennsylvania's pioneers. Regardless of its intent, it was clear to many that something needed to be done in the name of wildlife conservation in Pennsylvania.

There was a cultural divide in regard to conservation in the United States. Concerned citizens like the Lyman brothers and the previously mentioned Ohio residents wanted to preserve their local wildlife, while market hunters and fur traders were concerned about turning a profit, affluent travelers wanted a "hunt of a lifetime" experience and out-of-touch state lawmakers thought the extinction of certain animals was absurd nonsense. While hunters like Tome should not be viewed with harsh criticism, they were the embodiment of subsistence hunting becoming unsustainable for the natural ecosystem. In defense of the seemingly ignorant lawmakers, they were merely parroting the sentiments of William Penn. Shortly after he first arrived in Pennsylvania on October 29, 1682, he described the natural wealth of the commonwealth through his correspondence:

> The food, the woods yield, is your elks, deer, raccoons, beaver, rabbets, turkeys, pheasants, heath-birds, pigeons and partridge innumerably; we need no setting dogs to ketch, they run by droves into the house in cold weather….Our rivers have also plenty of excellent fish and water foul as sturgeon, roe shad, herring, catfish, or flatheads, sheeps heads, roach and perch; and trout in inland streames. Of foule, the swan, white, gray and black goose, and brands, the best duck and teal I ever eate and the snipe and curloe with the snow bird are also excellent…the elck as big as a small ox; deer, bigger than ours; very plentiful deer, beaver, raccoon and squirrels.[30]

Penn was not alone in recognizing the natural splendor of Pennsylvania. President Ulysses S. Grant made three fishing trips to Elk County, the heart of the Pennsylvania Wilds. His first trip was in 1869. He fished along the Clarion River not far from where Jacobs killed the last elk some years prior. During his first term as president, Grant visited Elk County again, this time a few miles below the village of Benezette to a town that now bears his name—Grant, Pennsylvania. In her *History of Elk County, Pennsylvania* published in 1981, Alice Wessman adamantly wrote that

> there is no doubt that President Grant enjoyed his short vacation in Bennetts Valley and that upon his return to Washington, he felt better able to cope with the tremendous responsibilities of the Presidency.[31]

Waterfall in the Forest by American artist George Hetzel. *1865.*

In a sense, Grant became a much better president because of his visit to the Pennsylvania Wilds.

Though Grant vastly enjoyed the natural splendor of Elk County, it was gravely threatened. What Penn considered unthinkable did eventually happen, and Pennsylvania's once natural beauty ran out. By the end of the nineteenth century, much of the wildlife that Penn described was either extinct or severely endangered. Due to an increase in the logging and coal mining industries throughout Pennsylvania, habitats were destroyed and waterways polluted—further hampering the necessary conditions for the great Pennsylvania wildlife to thrive. It would take a great deal of effort from both the citizens of Pennsylvania and the government to correct the great wrongs that had been done to the land for centuries.

2

CROSSCUT SAW

One of the first major enterprises that occupied the north-central Pennsylvania region was the lumber industry. It should be of no surprise that this business dominated the entire state, as Pennsylvania has always been a land of rich and vast forests. This was reflected early on through the name of the state, where -sylvania is derived from the Latin word *sylva*, meaning "forest." William Penn described the origin of the state's name in a letter to his friend Robert Turner in 1681 right after the charter for the commonwealth was issued by the king of England:

> *This day my country was confirmed to me under the great seal of England, with large powers and privileges, by the name of Pennsylvania, a name the king would give it, in honour of my father. I chose New Wales, being, as this, a pretty hilly country, but Penn being Welsh for a head…the highest land in England, called this Pennsylvania, which is, the high or head woodlands; for I proposed, when the secretary, a Welshman, refused to have it called New Wales, Sylvania, and they added Penn to it, and though I much opposed it, and went to the king to have it struck out and altered, he said it was passed, and would take it upon him; nor could twenty guineas move the under-secretaries to vary the name, for I feared lest it should be looked on as a vanity in me, and not as a respect in the king, as it truly was, to my father, whom he often mentions with praise.*[32]

It was clear from the beginning that Penn and King Charles II recognized how great the forests of Pennsylvania were. They were the head woodlands of the new world.

Penn also understood the need to conserve his *sylvania*. In 1681, he issued his Charter of Rights to settlers in which he attempted to lead a conservation effort, by ordering that there should be one acre of trees untouched for every five acres cleared.[33] While this proved effective in the early days of Pennsylvania's history, it would soon be ignored completely.

Many other early Pennsylvania settlers and historical American figures also praised the great wealth of the state's forestry. Gottlieb Mittelberger, a German pioneer who traversed Pennsylvania's wonderful forests, described some of the tree species that he observed during his travels in 1750:

> *Sassafras trees, which are not to be found in Europe, are plentiful here.... There are many sugar trees here which are as thick and high as an oak tree.... The beautiful tulip trees grow frequently there. In the month of May, when they are in blossoms, they are full of tulips; these look yellow and tabbie red, and are as natural as those that grow out of the ground. The trees are as thick and high as the tallest cherry trees.... The wood in the new country Pennsylvania grows fast and is much taller, but less durable than with us. It is quite surprising how dense the forests are, and what beautiful, smooth, thick and tall trees they contain. There are many kinds of trees, mostly oaks, but they are not so fruitful as those in Germany.... Walnut trees are exceedingly plentiful; this beautiful coffee-brown and hard wood is precious and useful, because all sorts of fine and elegant household furniture are made of it. When cut, a great deal of it is shipped to Holland, England, Ireland and other countries where it brings a high price.[34]*

Mittelberger goes into further detail about the plentiful chestnut, wild cherry, cedar and white pine trees. He also alluded to the future economic value that the forest contained. Many other pioneers also recognized the value within the state's timber supply.

Described in a 1770 account from his personal journal, George Washington admired the scenery of Pennsylvania's forestry while on an expedition down the Ohio River:

> *This tract, which contains about one thousand six hundred acres, includes some as fine land as ever I saw, and a great deal of rich meadow; it is well watered, and has a valuable mill-seat.... The lands which I passed over*

Forest Interior by American artist Ralph Blakelock depicting forests in Appalachia. *Late nineteenth century.*

today were generally hilly, and the growth chiefly white oak, but very good notwithstanding; and what is extraordinary and contrary to the property of all other land I ever saw before, the hills are the richest land; the soil upon the sides and summits of them being as black as coal, and the growth walnut and cherry.[35]

About a month later, on the same expedition, Washington offered another account of the terrain:

The land between the Mingo town and Pittsburg is of different kinds. For four or five miles after leaving the first mentioned place, we passed over steep, hilly ground, covered with white oak, and a thin, shallow soil. This was succeeded by a lively white oak land, less broken; and this again by rich land, the growth of which was chiefly white and red oak, mixed; which lasted with some interval of different ridges, all the way to Pittsburg.[36]

Philip Tome also provided a vivid description of Pennsylvania's lumber. In this context, his account is more important than Washington's and Mittelberger chronicles because Tome reported from the regions specifically in north-central Pennsylvania where the elk herd currently resided. Tome assessed the land as follows:

My first elk-hunting in this region was in 1816, and I continued it for five years. During this time I traveled over every part of this section of Pennsylvania and New York, and became familiar with the country between the Allegany and Susquehannah. In a circuit of ten miles around the head of the Tionesta, I thought the pine timber was better than in any other part of the region I have mentioned. The timber region commenced about seven miles from the Allegany River, two miles above Warren. The southeast branch heads in a good farming country, covered with beech, maple, chestnut, and some scattering wild-cherry trees, some of which later measured three feet in diameter, and not a branch within fifty feet of the ground. Here were also white-wood trees, four feet in diameter, with the lower limbs sixty feet from the ground. The country around the mouth of the creek was covered with a magnificent growth of pine and oak. Hence to the head of Willow Creek is a good farming country.[37]

Tome's description of the region aligns itself with the accounts of both Washington and Mittleberger, thus showing the breadth and quality of

Pennsylvania's forests. Tome claimed that some wild cherry trees in this region did not have a branch within fifty feet of the ground, underscoring the enormous stature of some of the ancient relics within the virgin forests of the state. Toward the end of his account, Tome hinted at the great value in the land as a potentially prosperous farming country. It was during this time that the first families of Elk County established permanent residencies along the Bennetts Branch of the Sinnemahoning River in what is now Jay and Benezette Townships.

The health of Pennsylvania's forests directly affects the health of its wildlife. The forests are the habitat of the elk, white-tailed deer, black bear, song and insectivorous birds, cottontail rabbits and all other species. Therefore, in order to protect and preserve the native animals, the forests would need to be managed in an effective and environmentally conscious manner. However, the Pennsylvanians of the nineteenth century failed to see the environmental ramifications that the lumber industry posed until it was too late. Fueled by economic incentives in an unregulated market, many capitalized on the profitability of the industry. It would take over one hundred years for Pennsylvanians to learn and implement sustainable forest management techniques.

It is clear, through the commentary of Mittelberger, Washington and Tome, that the land was filled with a natural abundance and wealth of timber, which, as alluded to by Mittelberger, could provide Europe and the Americas with new wood products on a level never seen before. This is what attracted Pennsylvania's first settlers, who were primarily lumbermen. In the mid-nineteenth century, John Leander Bishop, a historian on American manufacturing, provided accounts of the state's earliest sawmills. These mills were founded in the late seventeenth century by the Dutch and the Swedes a few years before Penn first set foot in Pennsylvania.

In reference to a mill existing a few years later on "Carcoon Creek," it was represented to the Upland Court, in March 1678, that in consequence of the land being daily taken up around it, it would soon be left destitute of timber, and the Court therefore ordered 100 acres of land to be appropriated for its use. The Swedes also had a mill supposed to have been a sawmill, in Frankford, before the landing of Penn....A sawmill appears to have been built for the use of the colony by the first settlers under the Proprietary, soon after their landing. In a letter to the Free Society of Traders in 1683, giving an account of Pennsylvania, William Penn alludes to their sawmill for timber.[38]

Many others soon saw the value in Pennsylvania's timber and quickly built sawmills throughout the state. In 1791, John Lincklaen, an officer in the Dutch navy and agent of the Holland Land Company, wrote about his experiences visiting a Pennsylvania sawmill:

> *Samuel Preston, quaker, and manager of Mr. Drinker's land, received us very politely in his log house, and gave us bacon and good chocolate. He began the Stockport* [now in Wayne County] *settlement two years ago— he has now two sawmills and another gristmill....He employs from 20 to 30 workmen both for his mills and for cutting roads of communication.*[39]

The sawmills described by Lincklaen were a source of economic prosperity for the community of Stockport. The workers relied on the lumber industry as a source of income for their families. The innate profitability was underscored by the access to luxury items that Lincklaen received: bacon and chocolate. In addition, lumber mills were a main reason for the construction and development of Pennsylvania's early infrastructure. The products from these mills needed to be shipped elsewhere to be sold. Often mills were built near water so that the logs could be floated downstream, or roads were constructed throughout the towns so that land transportation was a viable option.

Throughout the late eighteenth and early nineteenth centuries, sawmills from Philadelphia to Pittsburgh were erected. Chief Cornplanter, a personal friend of Philip Tome's, owned and operated a mill in Warren

Stereoscopic photograph of a sawmill in Williamsport, Pennsylvania. *Library of Congress, 1860–90.*

County. Jefferson County's first settler, Joseph Barnett, erected the first sawmill in the area. Traveling from Dauphin County, he, with the help of nine of Cornplanter's tribesmen, constructed the mill where Sandy Lick Creek and Mill Creek join, forming Red Bank Creek. Additionally, McKean County had a grist and sawmill erected in 1798 by a Mr. King at a town then called Ceres.[40]

By the early nineteenth century, some of Pennsylvania's only remaining virgin forests resided in its north-central region, specifically in Elk, Cameron and Potter Counties. In 1832, Potter County, known for its great white pines, was still nearly untouched forest. At that time, there was scarcely an inhabitant for every six hundred acres of its area. It contained an abundance of oak, walnut, sugar maple, beech, whitewood and pine.[41] According to Alice Wessman, Elk County in 1843 was, for the greater part of its area, "still covered with primitive forest," which consisted principally of white pine.[42] Sawmills in Elk County can be traced back about twenty years prior. The first mill is reported to have been erected by Zebulon Warner at Caledonia; James L. Gillis built one on Big Mill Creek in 1822; and Enos Gillis, his brother, had a sawmill in Ridgway by 1826.[43] Caledonia and Ridgway played vital roles in the history of Elk County. Caledonia was the site of the first county courthouse until it was moved a few years later to Ridgway, where it still is today. These and the mills that followed would help launch the lumber industry throughout Bennetts Valley.

A significant portion of the lumber from the Bennetts Valley region was floated down various waterways into Williamsport, Pennsylvania, which was known for over thirty years as the lumber capital of the nation. In fact, the massive pine trees of the area were used as mast poles on sailing ships built across the country.

Much of the land in the north-central region was owned by the Holland Land Company. Due to the rugged terrain and lack of connection from major cities, the company's landholdings were slow to sell. This prompted the company to employ lumberman and ironworker Peter Pearsall to survey the land and engineer and build sawmills in the region. In 1817, Pearsall discovered the large, impenetrable tracts of white pine, hemlock, oak, hickory and chestnut trees that covered the rolling hills of north-central Pennsylvania. Eventually, Pearsall moved his family to Sinnemahoning and then Caledonia, where he constructed and operated sawmills on behalf of the Holland Land Company.[44]

In 1811, Thomas Walter Dent III emigrated from England to settle an area several miles from Driftwood. He married Elizabeth Fush Overturf,

Before trains came to Dents Run, the easiest way to transport timber was to float the logs downstream. *Courtesy of Mt. Zion Historical Society.*

whose family was the second to come to reside in Driftwood. To this family, Miles Dent was born. This man, at the age of twenty-three, purchased several thousand acres of virgin timber that extended from the confluence of Dents Run to Bell Draft. Miles maintained a logging camp, railroad and multiple roads so that he could harvest timber on the top of the mountain. Logs were pulled by horses to the camp; bigger logs were spared and built into rafts and floated down the Bennetts Branch to Williamsport. In 1870, Dent floated his last timber down the river when he built the first steam-powered sawmill in the area.[45]

Another one of the first families to inhabit this area was the Mix family. Located between Dents Run and Driftwood, Amos Mix and his wife, Clarinda, settled in what is now known as Mix Run. The Mixes were lumbermen and outdoorsmen, but their claim to fame came via their connections to a vast network of influential American figures. Tom Mix, a direct descendant of Amos Mix, eventually moved to Hollywood and became a famous cowboy and western movie star. In a detailed history of the Mix family and other pioneers of the Bennetts Branch, historian James Burke claimed that Amos Mix was related to Presidents Millard Fillmore, Rutherford B. Hayes, Gerald Ford and John F. Kennedy. Additionally, Burke asserted that Amos Mix could claim to be an ancestor of many influential writers, actors and prominent American figures like John Wayne, Robert Frost, Walt Disney, Ralph Waldo Emerson and Eli Whitney.[46]

Other pioneers inhabited nearby regions with the same goal of striking it rich in the lumber industry. In 1827, the brothers, Reuben, Ebenezer and Carpenter Winslow purchased 380 acres of land now known as Winslow Hill.[47] Frederick Weed founded the village of Weedville in 1817 and built the town's first sawmill in 1820.[48] Revolutionary War veteran Isaac Webb founded Webb Town, now known as Force, sometime between 1809 and 1818. He purchased nearly one thousand acres and built a sawmill, gristmill and general store.[49]

Inhibited by a pre–Industrial Revolution lack of technology, these mills had small effects on the ecosystem of the area, although commercial logging would soon prove otherwise. That, however, did not reach Jay and Benezette Townships until 1848, when, in Medix Run, a New England–based factory became the principal lumbering center for Bennetts Valley.[50]

The value of timber harvested in Pennsylvania between 1840 and 1870 increased from little over $1 million to nearly $29 million. Between 1860 and 1870, the state led all others in the production of saw timber.[51] The growth in production was enabled chiefly by the introduction of the railroad throughout Pennsylvania, which accelerated the logging industry's ability to distribute its product. In 1874, the Allegheny Valley Railroad was completed from Driftwood to Red Bank, giving Jay and Benezette Townships direct access to the Pittsburgh market.

The profitability for the lumber industry increased throughout this region and, as a result, attracted more companies to purchase land and invest in sawmills of their own. In 1895, the mill in Medix Run was the second largest in Elk County, turning out 35 million feet of lumber yearly. Soon thereafter in 1902, the Goodyear Company purchased the mill, a small nearby railroad and approximately twenty thousand acres of timber with an estimated 350 to 500 million feet of hemlock and hardwood yet to be harvested. The newly acquired land resided within Elk, Cameron and Clearfield Counties—the modern-day heart of Pennsylvania's Elk Country.

Throughout the nineteenth century, the lumber industry evolved from an archipelago of sawmills in infant communities spanning the entire state into massive tree harvesting industries that propelled Pennsylvania to the

This photographic plate of an elk was taken from a larger series by Eadweard Muybridge titled *Animal Locomotion*. The collection includes hundreds of similar photographs meant to document animal movement. *1887*.

forefront of timber production in the country. The early days of lumber production did not pose a great threat to the state's wildlife because it was done at a moderate pace. With the invention of the steam engine came a faster way to ship products, and as the industry grew, the production process became more efficient and streamlined.

As the harvesting of Pennsylvania's lumber grew at an exponential pace, the negative effects on the wildlife were quickly seen. Elk typically relied on heavy forest growth during the summer months for shade and protection. Now, their habitat was being taken away from them at an unadaptable rate. It is no coincidence that the last elk was killed by Jim Jacobs in the 1860s when the lumber industry was at its peak. By leveling the state's forests, the elk had lost a major source of protection and were now more susceptible to being spotted by hunters. Clear-cutting the forests made hunting that much easier, which resulted in the devastation of not only Pennsylvania's forests but also its wild game.

Where wildlife populations were at an all-time low, Pennsylvania's residents were seeing prosperous economic gains. The profitability of the forests in the north-central region attracted many people from across the state to seek employment in the local lumberyards. Due to the increase in population and economic sustainability, the residents had started to form real communities—consisting of churches, schools, stores and hotels—for the first time in the region's history.[52]

Peter Pearsall was directly responsible for the construction of one of the first churches in Bennetts Valley. In 1832, Pearsall donated land from his farm to be used for the construction of a Baptist church; it would later shift to a Methodist faith in order to better service the community. Unfortunately, Pearsall passed away in 1838, leaving the plans to build the church as a faded dream. Pearsall's son Alfred sought to fulfill his father's goal and spearheaded the initiative to have it constructed. Mary Emery, Alfred's daughter and Peter's granddaughter, provided the following account on her family's influence on the church:

> The church was originally started with donations he (Alfred Pearsall) gave liberally. When I was a small child, I accompanied the Committee down to grandfather's old mill in search of stones for the foundation. I have always been proud of my grandfather. Father boarded the carpenters until the building was enclosed....It was not plastered until 1856. In the fall of 1859, there was a protracted meeting held there which was very successful in bringing in the delinquents. Father said as they knelt they were so intent upon Salvation that the peaches rolled out of their pockets, for the church stood in the midst of a peach orchard, and in the springtime, when the trees were in bloom, the place was one of the most beautiful imaginable, while the fruit was ripe, it seemed as if everyone was free to help himself....In regards to peaches, father said it was grandfather's plan to plant a fruit tree in every corner and along the fences of the farm, that everyone should be welcome to what fruit they wanted to eat....I very much doubt that they would have ever finished the church had it not been for father.[53]

It was clear that Peter Pearsall sincerely wanted to give back to the region that brought his family great wealth. Peter's passion inspired his son Alfred to complete the church, and as a result, the building provided a safe haven to all in the community.

The church at Mt. Zion was not the only religious establishment in the area. By 1858, there were four Methodist churches within Jay and Benezette Townships. St. Cecilia, a catholic church in Benezette, was built in 1879. Throughout the rest of the century, three more Methodist churches were built in Benezette, Grant and Winslow Hill. Families were settling the areas in search of employment and as a result needed places of worship. The creation of these churches was a sign of the first great population expansion in Bennetts Valley.[54]

Schools that were founded in the area further prove this point. By 1901, there were seven schools in operation in Jay Township: the Paine School

Mt. Zion Church, the oldest protestant church in Elk County, burned down in 1976. *Courtesy of Mt. Zion Historical Society.*

near Fairview, the Pike School and Mountain School on Mt. Zion, the Webb School near Weedville, the Spring Run School, the Gray School was located at the intersection of Gray Hill and Rock Hill and the Caledonia School. During the same period, another five schools were in operation in Benezette Township. In 1821, Cephas Morey built the first school in Medix Run. The other four schools opened soon thereafter: the Huston School was located in the northeast corner of the township, the Mt. Pleasant school resided on top of Winslow Hill, a two-room school building existed in Dents Run and another school was in operation in Benezette. Churches and schools flooded the eastern portion of Bennetts Valley, highlighting social development and economic growth.[55]

In the late 1830s, Philip Tome commented on the increased proliferation of the lumber industry in north-central Pennsylvania, specifically in McKean County, about an hour drive north of the Valley. Tome mentioned how two local entrepreneurs, a Mr. Irvin and Edwin Sanderson, erected an extensive sawmill near Willow Creek. The two founders were also backed by a Mr. Clark of Vermont who provided funding for the venture, further showing that the region was deemed a profitable endeavor by those residing far from the state. Tome proclaimed that the new sawmill was the most extensive

> *in that section of country, to be driven by steam, in addition to two good mills they now have, driven by water power. They are the owners of about seventeen thousand acres of excellent land, covered with pine, hemlock, maple, beech, chestnut, and oak.*[56]

Tome directly attributed the construction and future success of this operation with technology made available via the Industrial Revolution. Without the invention of the steam engine, these new mills would not be nearly as efficient as they were. Tome went on to describe the economic impact of this business venture:

> *They are also building a plank road four miles in length, from their mills to the river. They paid in cash for their land, over seventy thousand dollars, and are paying cash for everything they require in building, thereby doing great good to the inhabitants of the neighborhood—more than any establishment on the Allegany. They have also built a number of dwelling-houses and barns. The steam mill is expected to saw about thirty-five thousand feet of lumber per hour. They intend building this year a railroad through their land, which, with buildings to be erected, will furnish employment for a large number of persons. Corydon, at the mouth of Willow Creek, is a flourishing village, chiefly owing to the enterprise of the gentlemen above named.*[57]

According to Tome's estimation, the new sawmill provided multiple forms of direct economic relief to the incredibly rural area. Paying in cash for all of the land and construction costs, the founders ensured that the money would remain local to the area. In addition, the mill was directly responsible for the creation of all local major infrastructure. Mills needed to transport their product to the urban centers of Pennsylvania. This mill more than likely sent shipments to the Pittsburgh area or in some cases Buffalo, New York. By establishing the infrastructure to send their goods to these cities, they also enabled the local population to become interconnected with nearby areas, bolstering their trade economy. Finally, the new mills created jobs. which brought more people to the region in search of employment.

Mr. Irvin was considered to be the wealthiest person in this region at the time. Owning large swaths of land, a valuable gristmill, a woolen factory, an iron foundry, the Cornplanter Hotel (named after Chief Cornplanter of the Seneca nation) and a store, in addition to the new sawmill, allowed Irvin's wife to give back to the region from which they directly profited. Tome described Mr. Irvin's wife in the following manner:

> *His wife was a most exemplary woman, devoting her whole life to deeds of benevolence. Her active charity did not stop with feeding and clothing all the destitute within her reach, but she was mindful of their spiritual wants, and opened a Sabbath School in her own house, bringing in all in the vicinity. Among her other good deeds she built at a cost of four thousand dollars, a stone church for the Presbyterian congregation of which she was a member. Her earthly labors ended soon after its completion, the first sermon ever delivered in it being upon the occasion of her funeral, and her remains were the first laid in the adjoining graveyard. She was universally lamented, and will long live in the memory of those who knew her, as one of those upon whom the bestowal of wealth is a blessing to all within their influence.*[58]

Mr. Irvin's wife destroyed the common Gilded Age stereotype that industrial giants of the period cared solely about profit and nothing about the surrounding neighborhoods. While this stereotype was surely true in other aspects of the country, Mrs. Irvin proved that not every business venture during the era was operated with pure malevolence.

The next biggest concern for the new mill was the effect it had on the local wildlife and ecosystem. Tome contended that "the lands of these gentlemen still abound with bears and deer, furnishing fine ground for the hunter."[59] However, his observations came too early and do not accurately describe the full ramifications of the mill's presence. While there is scientific evidence that supports the notion that certain forestry practices benefit elk and deer populations, the same cannot be said for other species relying on the habitat that was being destroyed.

The increased profitability in lumber production and subsequent growth of community in many regions in north-central Pennsylvania did not come without a cost. The state's natural forests and habitats were being destroyed. Wild forest fires, massive floods and soil erosion left behind scenes of unbelievable devastation. A vast region within north-central Pennsylvania became known as the "Pennsylvania Desert." This distinction was given to the area in 1923 by Gifford Pinchot, the governor of Pennsylvania at the time, who wrote, "The one word which properly describes the facts surrounding the forest and lumber situation in Pennsylvania is 'bare.'"[60]

The destruction of America's forests was seen firsthand during the late nineteenth and early twentieth centuries. *Farm Security Administration, 1935.*

Pinchot is well regarded as the father of American forestry. While he did not invent the concept, he helped make it a widely accepted practice. Pinchot described how many people viewed the work of forestry during the late nineteenth century: "What talk there was about forest preservation was no more effective than the buzzing of a mosquito, and about as irritating to the promoters." He claimed to have asked C.S. Sargent, one of the leading contemporary academics on forestry, why he had omitted any talk of handling the forest crop in a sustainable manner from his scholarship. In response, Sargent ignorantly added that "he had put into the book all that there was to know."[61]

It appeared as if no one worried about the pitfalls that a lack of meaningful forestry practices would create. Even state-sponsored forestry organizations neglected to see any potential benefits from forest conservation practices. Pinchot claimed that a quotation from the New York State Forest Commission's report of 1886 accurately described how forestry was severely looked down on:

> *Those who understand the science of forestry as it exists in Europe, and are familiar with the methods that obtain and the character of the foresters employed there, need not be told that at the present time it would be equally*

Left: Portrait of Gifford Pinchot taken by Underwood & Underwood. *Library of Congress, 1921.*

Right: President Theodore Roosevelt (*left*) and Chief Forester Gifford Pinchot (*right*) on the river steamer *Mississippi* during a trip of the Inland Waterways Commission down the Mississippi River. *Library of Congress, 1907.*

> *as vain to endeavor to employ the methods of European forest science for our State purposes as it would be to try to find the ideal European educated forester in the North Woods.*[62]

However, if the landscape of Pennsylvania and the rest of the country were to survive in addition to the wildlife that the forests harbored, Pinchot and his followers would have to take control of the public narrative.

During the latter half of the nineteenth century—and due in large part to the lumber industry—the forest fires that swept through north-central Pennsylvania started to become a massive financial and humanitarian crisis. According to a report to the secretary of the Department of Agriculture from the 1896 issue of the *Philadelphia Inquirer*, the first state forestry commissioner, Dr. J.T. Rothrock, wrote the following statement in regard to the financial strain caused by Pennsylvania forest fires:

> *The most obvious consequences of forest fires, serious as they may be, are by no means, of the greatest importance. Loss of logs, of bark, of standing timber, young and old, of fences and occasionally buildings, is not less than a million dollars annually to this Commonwealth. This might well enough be termed a direct loss to the State. The indirect, or the consequential damages to the State is many times greater.[63]*

The most consequential damage that Rothrock referenced was the destruction of the future timber industry. Forest fires burning young and developing areas would prove to be detrimental to the state and future economic gains for the region. Rothrock continued to claim that the profits lost from timber areas from forest fires would "be worth not less than $1,200,000,000" in forty years. Adjusted for inflation, Rothrock's appraisal of the Pennsylvania lumber industry would be the equivalent of approximately $40 billion today.

Accompanying Rothrock's report is a statement by his clerk Robert S. Conklin (who would later become a commissioner for the Department of Forestry) that went in depth to describe the destruction caused by forest fires that year:

> *An approximate estimate from reports at hand establishes the fact that in the year 1895 there were about 225,000 acres of woodland burned over, occasioning a great loss of valuable timber, aggregating fully $1,000,000. Many fences were destroyed and about 5,000 men were engaged a total of about 250 days in extinguishing the fires, representing a wage account to the farming community of about $45,000. The lumbering interests reports have not been received as yet. Twenty buildings were destroyed, among which were several sawmills. Two men and five horses and cattle lost their lives in the fires. Much cut and sawed timber was also burned.[64]*

Laws punishing those responsible for forest fires had already been established long before Rothrock and the Department of Forestry. In 1867, an act firmly established penalties for setting forest fires in Clearfield, Fulton and Elk Counties. It also extended the statute of limitations to six years. Union County established a similar law that imposed fines and terms of imprisonment for offenders. However, this act included in its preamble the precise motives associated with the passing of the law:

> *Whereas, There being certain mountain and other wild lands in the county of Union which are fired from year to year, thereby destroying the young*

timber and causing the land to be worthless for the purpose of timber: And whereas, Should such young timber not be destroyed it would add to the value of the land, in the course of twenty years, from fifty to one hundred dollars per acre, thus increasing the wealth of the county thousands of dollars, therefore, etc.[65]

This law uttered the sentiment that Rothrock would eventually hold: young timber fields needed to be preserved and protected. Additionally, those in power were establishing these laws to specifically protect future economic gains. Altruistic motivations were often auxiliary in practice.

By 1895, Pennsylvania had experienced a sharp decrease in the percentage of forested areas, from 90 percent of the state's acreage to approximately 36 percent. Of the state's land base of 44,817 square miles, at least 4,716 had become wastelands and an additional 4,000 square miles of farmland had been abandoned because of degradation. The needy state of Pennsylvania's forests is what inspired Rothrock to become a leader in the field of forestry.

Rothrock was born in McVeytown, Pennsylvania, in 1839. He obtained his undergraduate degree from Harvard and eventually received a medical degree from the University of Pennsylvania. Throughout his life, Rothrock was always fond of the outdoors; he believed that the forests were a natural healing remedy to everyone. "Remove the forests and you remove the factor that makes the air fit to breathe," he wrote.

Working as both a botanist and a surgeon, Rothrock garnered respect and influence in many different professional circles. In 1875, he received an appointment to the University of Pennsylvania as a professor of botany. Five years later, Rothrock left and studied in Germany under renowned botanist Anton DeBary at the University of Strasbourg. Rothrock sought to learn advanced forestry techniques that had become well established throughout Europe. German forestry techniques were principally focused on economic interests, promoted through the scientific and mathematical ordering of the forests. The meticulous and careful planning of forests was an alien concept within the United States.[66]

What made Rothrock well known and revered was his ability to take the advanced scientific concepts that he learned throughout his life and translate them into layman's terms to the people of Pennsylvania. Early forestry and later conservation efforts were born from highly educated elites that had the means to afford these advanced studies. Many of the important figures in Pennsylvania's early environmental history possessed advanced degrees of some sort. In a sense, the educated and wealthy were the only people who

Joseph Trimble Rothrock was always known for his love of nature and Pennsylvania's forests. *Library of Congress, 1919.*

could afford to care about conservation efforts and, by extension, were the only people who could afford to care about Pennsylvania's wildlife.

In 1893, Rothrock left the University of Pennsylvania and led an investigation into the factors affecting Pennsylvania's forests. His report discussed timber production, land value, wastelands, taxation issues, ways to educate the public on the propagation of trees and forestry-restorative measures that could be undertaken. Rothrock's work culminated on March 15, 1895, when he presented an extensive 361-page report to the Pennsylvania House of Representatives. Wanting to demonstrate that "the safety of the State and of its interests required a change in existing [forestry] methods," Rothrock demanded action from the state legislature. Through his extensive research, organized presentation and passion for the health of the forests, he was able to convince the legislature to create a Division of Forestry within the Department of Agriculture, which reported to the Pennsylvania Forestry Commission. Additionally, he was appointed commissioner of that division. Lawmakers believed that such a novel and complex subject needed translators for the public and government, which made Rothrock the perfect leader.[67]

While Pennsylvania began to make major commitments to sustainable forestry practices, that did not absolve all of the damage that had been caused and was still wreaking havoc across the state. Bennetts Valley, too, did not avoid any of the calamity that plagued all of Pennsylvania.

Medix Run, being a principal lumbering town in the Valley, was subject to its own fair share of destruction from forest fires. Historian Thomas T. Taber III is a well-known scholar of the commercial logging industry in Pennsylvania and wrote extensively about the logging operations in Medix Run. He chronicled the series of destructive events that occurred in the logging town during the era when the Goodyear Lumber Company owned and operated the main mill of the town:

> *Medix Run was the scene of one conflagration after another. Possibly no other mill town had as many. In 1898 the company store of the shingle mill burned; in 1899 the kindling wood factory burned; in 1901 the company store of the lumber company burned; in December 1904 the tannery was destroyed in a quarter million dollar fire; in 1905 the Commercial Hotel burned and in a separate blaze a home was completely lost; and in June 1909 the mill burned and during the same month forest fires burned over a large area destroying logs and bark.*[68]

Eventually, a smaller mill was erected in the wake of the fire of 1909. However, the financial burdens imposed on the area proved to be too much for the Goodyear Lumber Company, and in 1912, the last piece of lumber was cut.

Another account, published in the *Philadelphia Inquirer* on May 18, 1896, detailed forest fires near Clearfield, an area just south of Jay and Benezette Townships. "Forest fires are still raging in many places throughout this county," read the article. It claimed that McGee's Saw Mill was the source of the fire and that five houses, a church and a hotel, located four miles from the mill, all burned down. Additionally, it stated that the town of Barrett was "entirely surrounded by a big woods which is a roaring furnace."

One of the men sent out to combat the fire saved a big sawmill belonging to Joseph Shaw and reported that 120,000 feet of logs were burned in the destruction.[69] The north-central region of Pennsylvania, the heart of the state's lumber industry, experienced many hardships that were a direct result of the logging industry. The forest fires were not only a threat to the profitability of the land but also severely endangered the people and wildlife that resided in logging communities. Even though the elk were extinct at

A Forest Fire: North America, by German artist Johann Friedrich Wilhelm Wegener. *1848.*

this point, the devastating effects reverberated through the white-tailed deer, small mammal and bird populations.

Rothrock attributed the forest fires to many different causes. Some were natural reasons. For example, lightning combined with arid weather could strike at a moment's notice. However, a lot of blame was easily attributed to human factors such as farmers who set fires to prepare the land for feeding pastures. Even more at fault was the lumber industry itself. Fires started from accidents within the sawmills, trees caught fire from railroad sparks and timber thieves ignited patches of forest to hide evidence of their work. "Almost every forest fire is the result of ignorance, carelessness, or crime, and that there is someone to punish for it," claimed Rothrock. For years, he lobbied for fire legislation as a forestry commissioner; he viewed the legislation as the "principal preventive 'essential' to forestry." The fires ravaged forests and left the soil barren; that was a crime against the people of Pennsylvania and future generations.[70]

Soon after the destruction wrought by fires, many violent floods swept through areas near large rivers. One of the main functions that forests have in a local environment is to hold back and retain water that would otherwise be absorbed into surrounding watersheds. Due to their incredible

Emporium Lumber Company's hardwood mill in Austin, Pennsylvania, after a flood. *1911.*

amount of foliage, trees hold and store a significant volume of water from the local environment. If a large section of forest is suddenly removed from an ecosystem, a proportional amount of water that would have normally been absorbed by the trees leaves the area as either streamflow or seepage to deeper groundwater. When this occurs, the water level in surrounding watersheds increases at a substantial rate. This phenomenon is what Pennsylvania experienced in the late nineteenth century and is what caused these massive floods.[71]

In Rothrock's 1893 report to the Pennsylvania legislature, he firmly established the notion that healthy forests were essential to protecting people and wildlife. Rothrock argued that forests regulated and protected streams, reduced the height of floods, moderated extremes of low water and protected mountain slopes against increased soil wash.[72]

While Rothrock attempted to quickly educate the public on sustainable forestry, waves of destruction were still ongoing and could not be entirely prevented. On January 9, 1895, the Monongahela River flooded areas surrounding Pittsburgh. The damage done by the flood was estimated at about $500,000, which included wrecked coal barriers, flooded mills and filled-in mines. An article from the *Philadelphia Times* claimed,

> *All the iron mills along the banks of the Allegheny and the Monongahela rivers are under water and are closed down until the flood recedes. None of the railroads are blockaded, although the tracks of the Pittsburg and Western are under water in the Allegheny. While the total damage will aggregate a considerable amount, yet it will not approach the loss in the floods of 1884 and 1891.*[73]

The amount of damage the city incurred was massive, but the most frightening aspect of this short article is that it was written in an offhand way that indicates just how commonplace floods were at the time. By downplaying the current catastrophe as being less disastrous than the two previous floods, the author normalized these scenes of environmental destruction.

All of the streams west of the continental divide are directly connected to the same watershed that surrounds Pittsburgh. Therefore, one of the main causes of the floods in Pittsburgh was the lack of care given to the forests in north-central Pennsylvania.

Pennsylvania was not alone in its struggles to control forest fires and floods. In fact, France experienced similar problems during the mid-nineteenth century and was well underway in finding solutions. Between 1846 and 1856, the French government incurred approximately $50 million in damages from floods alone. In 1891, an unnamed writer from the *Pittsburgh Dispatch* read the French government's report and made the case that this story was of "immense value to Pennsylvania." The author argued,

> The state has an immense quantity of mountain land of such slight value for agriculture that a very small premium might make it profitable to pursue the enterprise of forestry. We have already reached that stage in the denudation of the slopes indicated by the violent floods which follow the spring thaws and the summer storms and the shrunken flow of our rivers during the protracted periods of pleasant weather. Many mountain slopes denuded of their valuable timber are now waste land with a scrub growth upon it which might be made of great value to coming generations. It would certainly be good policy for the State to follow the example of France and to offer premiums on the protection of our mountains from erosion, the more even distribution of drainage throughout the summer and a provision of timber for the next generation by the planting of forests on the mountain lands, now useful for little else.[74]

The author pulled on the same heartstrings that pushed Rothrock to fight for the establishment of the Forestry Commission.

After a little less than a full century of unregulated lumbering practices, Pennsylvania finally decided it was time to implement meaningful forestry protocols. These efforts would strike the much-needed balance between conservation of wildlife and the preservation of local environments with the economic gains of the lumbering industry.[75]

Where Rothrock led the push for forestry in Pennsylvania, Gifford Pinchot emerged as the nation's preeminent leader on the same subject. The 1890s proved to be a major decade for forest conservationists. Pinchot claimed that systemic forestry in America began in North Carolina in 1892 and that

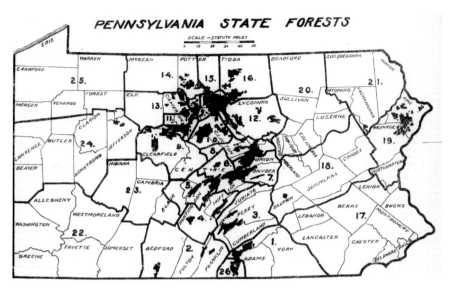

By the turn of the century, the newly minted Pennsylvania Department of Forestry had started to acquire and protect lands for State Forests. *Pennsylvania Department of Forestry, 1901.*

national interest "had its start in 1896 when Hoke Smith, Secretary of the Interior, asked the National Academy of Sciences to tell him what ought to be done with the national forest reserves and the public forest lands." The Forestry Committee strongly advised Hoke and President Grover Cleveland to create nearly twenty-two million acres of forest reserves. President Cleveland obliged. Then in 1898, the government introduced European-style forestry practices. "Instead of mere exhortation and viewing with alarm, the Division of Forestry of the Department of Agriculture offered to show timberland owners on the ground how to handle their lands for a second crop," claimed Pinchot. "That was a new thing in America."

Pinchot often argued that America's forests needed to be viewed as crops and that they must be protected for future generations of forests.

> *We must remember also that the forest is a crop. Using the word "agriculture" in its broad sense, a forest is an agricultural crop. Forestry then is a way of producing crops of wood from the soil, and therefore is tied with the production of all other crops.*[76]

The notion of timber cultivation being viewed as the growing and harvesting of crops was a new concept that Pinchot firmly believed in. Many Americans did not agree with him, and as a result, many forests were leveled and turned into deserts. Aligning the harvest of trees on the same spectrum as harvesting food crops is a tricky concept to grasp because of the length of time associated with their respective growing seasons. Profitable timber takes multiple decades to develop from seeds to full-grown trees. Juxtaposed against a prototypical agricultural product that is able to be produced in under a year, it was not intuitive to perceive trees in the same manner. Instead, America's forests were viewed largely as a resource that needed to be harvested without much thought being put to regenerate future crops. Rothrock related this ideology to "barbarism," and in a paper published by the American Philosophical Society in 1894, he wrote that two centuries of American inhabitance had

> *matured the tree-destroying tendency into an instinct....We furnish an illustration of a nation lapsing into the extravagance of barbarism because of the abundance of our supplies, so far at least as our use of the trees is concerned.*[77]

Although efforts to correct the harmful effects of commercial lumbering were well underway, the damage incurred by Pennsylvania's ecosystem was already done. Nearly every one of Pennsylvania's wildlife species would be severely affected. Birds are perhaps the most affected species of deforestation. They require mature forests as habitat for breeding,

The state's clear-cut wastelands came to be known as the Pennsylvania Desert. *Wikimedia Commons, photo taken before 1920.*

wintering and during migration. In addition, the presence of cavity trees, standing dead trees and logs on the forest floor are critical to many birds and small mammals. The lack of these ecological elements does not create a conducive environment for birds to live and prosper. Perhaps the ill-guided forestry practices in Pennsylvania were another contributor to the extinction of the passenger pigeon.[78]

Hares and rabbits were abundant in Pennsylvania and were economically important as small game. They feed by browsing and grazing and can benefit from an increase of low shrubs and herbs after timber harvesting, the abandonment of agricultural land and wildfire. Bill Freedman, the department chair of environmental science at Dalhousie University, claimed,

> *Most studies report that forest harvesting has relatively minor effects on small mammals. For example, no substantial differences were found in their overall abundance, species richness, or diversity among stands of mature forest, three- to five-year-old clear-cuts, strip-cuts, and shelterwood cuts.*

However, some medium-sized species, like marten, beaver and fisher, thrive in thick coniferous forests due to the complex biodiversity. Deforestation has been incredibly detrimental to these animal's continued survival.

Elk, however, may actually stand to benefit from forest harvesting practices. The primary source of nutrition for elk tend to be graminoids and forbs in spring, but they eat browse during the winter. Habitats created from timber harvesting and wildfire are the perfect environment for graminoids, forbs and browse to grow and thrive. White-tailed deer also benefit from this type of environment; in fact, the shrubby habitat supports deer even more than elk. In addition to providing the right kind of food, these grassy clearings give cover for deer and elk. However, with a deer population approaching dangerously low levels and an elk herd that had been hunted to extinction about thirty years prior, there would be almost no wildlife in Pennsylvania that could enjoy any potential upside from new forestry measures.[79]

The main motivation for the implementation of sustainable forest management procedures was protecting current and future economic value. For many years, Pennsylvanians viewed the forests as an asset that could easily be liquidated, and when their greatest source of income was nearly eradicated, leaders like J.T. Rothrock defended the commonwealth's ecosystem and Gifford Pinchot fought for conservation on the national stage. Additionally, Pennsylvania's reckless behavior toward the lumber industry wrought havoc in the forms of forest fires and floods, which threatened the safety and security of the state's residents. While rescuing the natural landscape is an admirable cause, it was not the overarching reason forestry practices were implemented. Instead, establishing a sustainable way to harvest timber that would protect future generations of wealth creation is what motivated many state and national lawmakers.

The lumber industry gave pioneers the ability to move to remote areas, erect sawmills and establish communities. As lumbering towns formed, communities found themselves firmly supplanted among them. Dotted with newly built churches, schools and stores, Pennsylvania was settled by people who wanted to stay. Unfortunately, the industry expelled much of the local wildlife. Those who wished to permanently reside in Pennsylvania, and see it thrive for generations to come, would need to make significant concessions toward a more sustainable way of living within the Pennsylvania Wilds.

3

A MOUNTAIN MAN'S DREAM

*B*y the end of the nineteenth century, what were once considered to be Pennsylvania's greatest natural resources—the vast forests and abundant wildlife—were on the verge of total annihilation. Concerned citizens across the state recognized this problem and formed private associations that would attempt to fix issues related to forestry and conservation in areas that the state government was failing to protect. As mentioned previously, J.T. Rothrock was the father of forestry in Pennsylvania. The devastating economic and rampant environmental destruction of Pennsylvania land was so explicit that the establishment of a state forestry commission was generally agreed on. That understanding of necessity was not present when it came to establishing a game commission.

Members of the State Sportsmen's Association, which met in early January 1893 in Harrisburg, were the first official advocates for the establishment of a game commission in Pennsylvania. According to an unnamed reporter from the *Lancaster Intelligencer*, the recommendations came from "the men who have the preservation and increase of game and fish most at heart." It was the goal of these sportsmen to create a conservation-based organization for Pennsylvania's wildlife, and as evidenced by the eradication of many species, it was obvious that a regulating body was needed. However, the same reporter described the recommendations of the Sportsmen's Association with much hesitancy:

> *Experience has taught us that enthusiasts demanding any particular legislation are apt to wander from the paths of common sense....There are, of course,*

some impracticable notions among the many urged by these eager sportsmen in convention assembled. The idea of restricting the number of deer that one individual may kill and the proposal to prevent the presence of dogs in regions inhabited by deer do not seem practicable. On the other hand, the thorough revision of the game protective laws is an evident necessity if some varieties are to be saved from absolute extermination, and the experiment of introducing Mongolian pheasants and prairie chickens is worth trying.[80]

The apprehension toward the regulation on deer harvests and using dogs to aid in hunting was well founded. Sustenance hunting was one of the main sources of food for rural residents of Pennsylvania in the nineteenth and even into the twentieth centuries. It is therefore reasonable for people to be against any measure that could severely affect their own ability to live. The reporter also referenced the greatly abused Scalp Act of 1883 as another reason for hesitancy; the act paid out bounties for the scalps of certain predatory species.

At the time, outlawing hunting dogs and implementing seasonal bag limits seemed like impractical measures that many could not reconcile. However, such methods are commonly accepted today. The author also recognized that game laws were needed in order to prevent "absolute extermination," which, luckily, would end up being the prevailing sentiment across the state.

Legislation surrounding wildlife conservation was a hot-button issue in 1895. The State Sportsmen's Association, wishing to push its agenda, found the support of House representative George Kunkel of Dauphin County. He introduced a bill proposing to establish a game commission in Pennsylvania. The first iteration of this bill resulted in defeat, but it was not a total loss for the association's conservation efforts. A different bill that prohibited the killing of deer in the state for the following five years did pass. Violating this law would result in a $200 fine. This would prove to be a useful tactic in preserving the Pennsylvania deer population, and it would not be the last time that the state would impose such restrictions. For the time being, the state legislature would rather enact game laws on its own rather than passing that responsibility onto another government agency.[81]

Soon, the state legislature passed a bill that banned the hunting of all game for the purpose of bartering or sale in Pennsylvania for the next two years. However, Governor Daniel H. Hastings vetoed it, claiming that

it would give a practical monopoly of the game of the State into the hands of the sportsmen, and prevent the fellow who enjoys the eating of it, but has not the skill to shoot it, from having any on his table.[82]

Elk Grazing on an Autumn Prairie by American artist George Catlin. *1846–48.*

It appeared as if the governor was conflicted on how his administration should approach its wildlife conservation policies. If the preservation of Pennsylvania's wild game species was truly a paramount issue, then Hastings should have signed this piece of legislation into law. Instead, he believed that all Pennsylvanians had an indelible right to benefit from the state's wildlife, even its commercialization. Hastings was unwilling to eliminate market hunting practices from Pennsylvania.

In June 1895, soon after the defeat of the anti–market hunting bill, a revised version of Representative Kunkel's game commission bill was passed and soon became law.[83] The year 1895 proved to be a progressive one for the state of Pennsylvania as far as its environmental legislation and associated agencies were concerned. Governor Hastings signed into law and established the Commission on Forestry, with J.T. Rothrock at the helm, as well as the Pennsylvania Game Commission. Hastings appointed what he believed to be six competent citizens to serve as the first game commissioners: William M. Kennedy, Allegheny City; Charles Heebner, Philadelphia; Irving A. Stearns, Wilkes-Barre; James H. Worden, Harrisburg; E.B. Westfall, Williamsport; and Coleman K. Sober, Lewisburg.[84]

Now that the board of commissioners had been established, an executive director needed to be appointed to lead the Pennsylvania Game

Commission. Sometimes referred to as the executive secretary, this position directly reported to the board of commissioners. After much deliberation, Dr. Benjamin Warren, avid environmental enthusiast and state zoologist, was appointed to the role.[85]

The first game commissioners had their work cut out for them. None of them were being paid a salary, and the game commission did not have any access to state funds. No compensation for the commissioners was an amendment to Representative Kunkel's bill that House Democrats demanded to be included in the legislation. During the first iteration, House Republicans refused to include the addition, subsequently causing the bill's vote to fail.

The commissioners were selected for the job because Governor Hastings believed that they would have the best interests of conservation at heart. If no salaries were being paid and little influential power was given to those in charge, then the positions would rarely be susceptible to corruption and only those truly interested in the greater cause of conservation would fill the positions. At the start, the only source of income that the Pennsylvania Game Commission had was from the sale of hunting licenses. Under these conditions, they were responsible for drafting and finalizing wildlife legislation that would be the foundation for the future of Pennsylvania.

Dr. Warren and commissioners Heebner and Worden led the committee that drafted the first legislation put forth by the Pennsylvania Game Commission. They pushed heavily for a ban on the sale and interstate transportation of Pennsylvania deer, wild turkeys, grouse and quail. In addition, it was proposed that a universal game season should be held to hunt all applicable species during a set time frame. However, the commission's first grand achievement in the field of conservation would not come until they were under the leadership of executive director Dr. Joseph Kalbfus.

Born on April 12, 1852, in Williamsport, Pennsylvania, Kalbfus came into the world during the most tumultuous time in regard to Pennsylvania's wildlife. In his early life, he was well aware of the extinction of many of Pennsylvania's native species, like the elk. As a young adult, he spent a number of years on the western plains during the dangerous frontier days. Throughout his travels, he observed game practices across much of the United States. In Kalbfus's autobiography, he discussed the treatment of big game in America's western frontier:

> *Because of my experience in the West I was able to tell almost unbelievable stories of how big game was being exterminated in the West and how*

not only individuals but even our National authorities were destroying our buffalo, elk, antelope, deer, and bear simply for profit or pleasure to a few and without regard for the rights of present and future generations. I was able to tell how men from the United States Army, as well as cowboys and Indian wards of the Nation, were gathered by hundreds at the expense of the Government, to add to the pleasure of Duke Alexis through the slaughter of innumerable buffalo and antelope; how these creatures were shot from railroad trains just to see them fall, and how men, both as individuals and banded together, were destroying the Nation's inheritance for profit to themselves simply because there was no law to prevent it.

As an illustration I used to cite the following as one of the many instances of this kind that came under my notice: When the grass began to turn green in the Spring following the hard Winter after the Chicago fire, four men came to camp on the Cache la Poudre and I visited them frequently. They were buffalo hunters and called themselves "the four Jacks." They told me that they, with one man as cook and four men as skinners, nine in all, had during the preceding Winter killed more than four thousand buffalo and had taken from their carcasses nothing but the hide, for which they got $2.00, the tongue, worth fifty cents, and such meat as they needed to eat. The rest of the animal was left to the wolves or to dry up on the ground.[86]

Hunters shooting buffalo from a train on the Kansas-Pacific Railroad. *Library of Congress, 1871.*

Kalbfus's experiences touring the American West and the Pennsylvania countryside shaped his political and ideological beliefs in regard to how conservation should be viewed. However, he was not always the leader of the Pennsylvania Game Commission. When he returned to Pennsylvania, he studied law and was admitted to the Carbon County Bar. He then served in government as a federal revenue officer and later became a member of the Pennsylvania state cabinet. He eventually left these roles to pursue his dream of becoming a dentist and opened up his own practice. Soon thereafter, the Pennsylvania Game Commission was formed, and Kalbfus was asked to become its executive director.

Since the position did not pay, Kalbfus was a dentist by day and game protector at night. He paid his own expenses because the game commission could not afford them. Throughout the early period of the commission's history, only wealthy professionals could afford to work as the executive secretary. Additionally, the position of game protector was by no means a popular one. In his autobiography, Kalbfus described the public sentiment shown toward game protectors during the late nineteenth century:

> In the very beginning I found that those engaged in the protection of game were not popular with the majority of the people of Pennsylvania who appeared to think that they had a constitutional right to carry guns when and where they pleased, and an inherent right to destroy game and birds at pleasure. By the average citizen Game Protectors were looked upon as men whose sole purpose in life was to annoy and prosecute honest people. Many, otherwise good citizens, could not see how any benefit could come because of protecting game and wild birds. They did their work well and to that end personally sacrificed both time and conservation. This was so simply because they did not understand what the birds were doing and what their life work meant to the people.[87]

While it was not an easy journey, Kalbfus stuck with the commission and, through his life's work, would become known as the father of conservation in Pennsylvania.

After nearly twenty years at the head of the organization, in his annual report published in 1914, Kalbfus publicly declared his motives and goals for the future of the game commission under his leadership:

> I believe for various reasons that hunting is a national necessity, that because this is so it is the duty of the State to supply to the fullest extent

*possible lands whereon men may hunt without running up against trespass
notices, and also to supply game of various kinds to be hunted. I believe
that sportsmen are better fitted to draft game laws than are scientists, or any
other class of men. Sportsmen in Pennsylvania today are not paupers; they
are supplying the money through which protection is given not only to game,
but also to song and insectivorous birds, and the sportsmen's ideas should be
given consideration in matters of this character.*[88]

Kalbfus adamantly believed that hunting needed to remain a staple
in Pennsylvania, for not only cultural but also conservation purposes.
Having grown up during the time in which Pennsylvania's wildlife was
severely threatened, Kalbfus was fully aware that overhunting was a main
cause for the endangerment of Pennsylvania's native species. He knew
that an important balance needed to be struck. The Pennsylvania Game
Commission had to be the arbiter of game laws that allowed hunting
practices but in a sustainable manner that would enable all current and
future residents to enjoy nature responsibly.

Kalbfus also noted that it was the duty of the state to supply the residents
of Pennsylvania with various game to be hunted. In the spring of 1905,
Pennsylvania's governor, Samuel Pennypacker, authorized the establishment
of game preserves for the protection of deer, wild turkey and other wildlife
not necessarily game animals. The goal of these locations was to rebuild and
provide security for Pennsylvania's wildlife. Hunting was strictly prohibited
in these areas. The first game refuge was established in Clinton County,
presently known as Sproul State Forest.[89]

By 1910, the Pennsylvania Game Commission had established three
refuges in the state. Joe Kosack, a Pennsylvania wildlife and conservation
historian, claimed that it was "a miniature version of Theodore Roosevelt's
grand national wild refuge plan."[90] The state land refuge system was the
impetus that revitalized many wild game and bird populations. These lands
sheltered the animals from predatory species and overzealous hunters.

Kalbfus was passionate about using the state refuge lands. He claimed
that he would often tour the lands during the beginning of hunting seasons
to ward off trespassing hunters. During the start of deer season in the
early 1900s, Kalbfus ran into a hunter during the early morning hours.
The hunter had chased a deer into the state refuge. Kalbfus met him at
the border, and while the hunter was dismayed at losing an opportunity
to harvest a deer, he understood the vital work the game commission
was doing.

Not every outdoorsman was as amiable as the hunter Kalbfus encountered. In fact, many hunters shared the sentiment that the Pennsylvania Game Commission was unjustly limiting their natural right to hunt. Game officers were often viewed as those looking to bully the honest man for no reason in particular. Throughout a significant portion of the commission's history, they would be looked at in infamy. The tension between conservation officers and hunters would only be fixed once the residents of the state could be properly educated on wildlife conservation policies and their effectiveness. It wouldn't be until the 1970s that the commission started to address public education as a primary concern.

No matter the obstacle posed by the common hunter, the Pennsylvania Game Commission was still making valiant and effective strides for preserving and protecting their wildlife. William T. Hornaday, a pioneer of American wildlife conservation, praised Pennsylvania's endeavors in this field:

> *Pennsylvania has been wide awake, and in advance of her times. I will cite her system of…game preserves as a model plan for other states to follow; and I sincerely hope that by the time the members of the present State Game Commission have passed from earth the people of Pennsylvania will have learned the value of the work they are now doing, and at least give them the appreciation that is deserved by public-spirited citizens who do large things for the People without hope of material reward.*[91]

The Pennsylvania Game Commission, under Kalbfus's leadership, was garnering national recognition.

Soon thereafter, another opportunity to revolutionize wildlife conservation would be available to Kalbfus and the rest of the commissioners. In 1913, Kalbfus and commissioner Dr. Charles Penrose, a renowned gynecologist and surgeon, purchased fifty elk from Yellowstone National Park. With the establishment of a game refuge system, the Pennsylvania Game Commission now had the means and the opportunity to reestablish Pennsylvania's once mighty elk herd.

During this time, Yellowstone's elk herd was expanding uncontrollably, and in order to counteract this, elk were being sold across the country. By 1912, the herd that resided in Yellowstone held a population of around thirty thousand. With civilization making its way into the area in tandem with the sudden population increase, the elk were running out of food. The most problematic area was in the Jackson's Hole region, located just south of Yellowstone. This fertile land was home to a significant portion of migrating elk in search of food during the winter months. However, many elk that came here struggled to find any form of sustenance. The *Philadelphia Inquirer* described the great struggle that the Jackson Hole elk endured just to avoid starvation in the following account from 1912:

> *In some instances they tore down the strongest barbed wire fences in search of food, so that many of the ranchmen were forced to pitch tents or make bivouacs near their haystacks, and to save the hay for their cattle were compelled to sleep by the stacks during the severest months of winter. Where the elk were too weak from starvation to make any fight against the barriers separating them from food, many of them simply lay down and died, whereupon the survivors would actually mount upon the fallen bodies of their companions and in this way reach a few morsels of hay. The settlers in Jackson's Hole did all they could to remedy the sufferings of the animals, often putting their own stock on extremely short allowance in order to do so.*[92]

The number of elk that would perish during the winter due to starvation in Jackson's Hole started to reach nearly one thousand annually. The State of Wyoming was dedicated to sustaining the elk population, so it attempted to feed the elk during the winter months, but it was becoming increasingly unfeasible. An appeal was eventually made to Congress, and President William Howard Taft signed a bill that gave $20,000 for elk rescue purposes. The federal monies were given to the U.S. Biological Survey, a government agency now known as the U.S. Fish and Wildlife Service. Extensive studies on the elk in Jackson's Hole were conducted, and some efforts were made to feed and protect the elk during the winter months. In spite of these federal endeavors, the death toll hovered around two thousand per year.[93]

After interventions from the Wyoming state and federal governments, a remedy to keeping the elk in and around Yellowstone was an unattainable ideal. In order to solve Yellowstone's elk problem, many of the elk from the Jackson's Hole region needed to be sold across the country. From 1912 to 1913, 195 elk were transported to the state of Washington; 40 to California; 50 to West Virginia; 80 to Arizona; 25 to Virginia, Colorado, Utah and other parts of Wyoming; 3 to South Dakota; and another 50 to state game refuges in Clearfield and Clinton Counties in Pennsylvania.[94] America's elk were being spread out across the country, and Pennsylvania was given a chance at redemption.

In what had to be a letter of pure excitement, Penrose wrote in February 1913 to Colonel Lloyd M. Brett, who oversaw Fort Yellowstone and had

Yellowstone has always been a natural wildlife and ecotourism destination. *William Henry Jackson, Library of Congress, 1871.*

commissioned the sale of the elk. In the letter, Penrose described the elk's current status:

> *The fifty elk captured under your supervision in Yellowstone Park for the State Forest Reserve of Pennsylvania, arrived in good shape a couple of weeks ago. Twenty-five elk have been placed in a reserve of about 50,000 acres in Clinton County, and twenty-five in a similar reserve in Clearfield County. They are now under fence in small enclosures and are being fed until the conditions are suitable to turn them loose in the late spring. If these elk do well, and are not an annoyance to the farmers during the winter, we hope to bring more of them here. As there have not been elk in Pennsylvania since the beginning of game protection, there is now no law protecting them, and we have before the Legislature an Act prohibiting the killing of elk for the next five years. The only matter about which I am doubtful is the damage that the elk may do during the winter, when their natural food is wanting. Of course, the Game Commission expects to feed them during the winter. I want to convey to you the thanks of the Pennsylvania Game Commission for your assistance in helping us to secure these animals.*[95]

One of Yellowstone's many elk, this animal still has velvet covering its antlers. *William Henry Jackson, Library of Congress, 1871.*

Additionally, twenty-two elk were purchased from a privately owned Monroe County facility in 1913. Twelve of the elk were released into state lands in Monroe County, and another ten were transported to a Centre County refuge. In all, seventy-seven free-roaming elk were released in Pennsylvania throughout 1913.[96]

For the first time since the last elk was slain by Jim Jacobs on the Clarion River in the 1860s, there were once again wapiti in Pennsylvania. Through decades of strong work in the field of conservation, the Pennsylvania Game Commission believed that the state was once again able to sustain one of America's most historic species and hoped to return them to their former glory.

A local magazine published an article titled, "Elk in Pennsylvania Once More: Howard Eaton Breaks All Records for Successful Transportation of Animals." Howard Eaton was the man personally responsible for the collection and transportation of the elk in Yellowstone. Not a single animal was harmed during transportation, and the article claimed that this was something that "government experts thought almost impossible" to achieve.[97]

However, it was not entirely certain that the elk population would be able to survive. Penrose claimed that they would need to be fed during the winter in addition to the pending prohibition on hunting legislation. Even though the elk that resided in Yellowstone were similar to the elk that once lived in Pennsylvania, it was no guarantee that they would be able to adapt to the different ecosystem.

By May 1913, just three months after the elk's arrival, Penrose reported to Colonel Brett that fourteen of the elk had become sick and died. The carcasses of the animals were sent to both Harrisburg and Philadelphia to be examined by state zoologists and veterinarians. No definite cause of death was ever determined, but the animals were found to be covered in moose ticks. While this was not confirmed to be the cause of any sickness or death, in response to the ticks, Penrose took action.

> We have dipped the elk in both preserves in an anti-tick preparation and they are now free of these insects and are apparently prospering. Notwithstanding the careful investigation that has been made, no one seems to know what killed the fourteen elk that have already died. I hope that we will lose no more.[98]

Colonel Brett eventually responded to the small epidemic and eased Penrose's concerns. He asserted that the ticks were most likely not the issue.[99] There was no direct cause of death found that could be attributed to those fourteen elk. For the time being, the remaining elk population was able to sustain themselves in the two reserves set up by the game commission, and no other apparent epidemic threatened their existence in the next decade.

It became clear early on that the restocking of the elk herd would not be a seamless transition. As Tome had described the elk a century prior, they were nomads of the forest, known to wander far from their territory. Some of the elk that were shipped to Pennsylvania traversed up to forty miles away from the release sites in less than a week. Like deer, elk also have a tendency to invade farmlands, destroying crops in the process. Kalbfus eventually relayed these concerns to the rest of the board of commissioners:

> They are not only disposed to wander far but also to raid, growing crops, and several claims for damage have already been filed. It seems to me that it would be well to wait a few years at least before releasing any more of these animals in the commonwealth.[100]

Crop damage and the elk's nomadic wandering would prove to be problems that the Pennsylvania Game Commission still faces today. Before the elk were reintroduced, many deer were shot in the name of crop destruction. If elk were to survive in Pennsylvania, then the death tolls from farmers would have to be severely limited. Kalbfus advised caution and patience to the board of commissioners; he wanted time to study the behavioral trends of the newly transplanted animals before making any further attempts to grow the population.

While elk may have been unpopular with nearby farmers, state-wide enthusiasm for the reintroduction of an extinct species was growing. Later in 1913, Milton S. Hershey, a Pennsylvania native and the founder of the Hershey Chocolate Company, purchased an elk statue to be placed at the entrance of Hershey Park. The amusement park was founded in 1906, and the statue welcomed every visitor from 1913 to 1978 until it was moved to the entrance of the newly built Zoo America, where it still stands today. Incorporating the elk as a paramount symbol of Hershey Park gave it an element of majestic prestige and awe.[101]

After residing in the state for a year, the initial Yellowstone elk herd proved that it could survive in Pennsylvania, and the majority of the board of game commissioners believed that it would be prudent to increase the sustaining population. In October 1914, going against the wishes of Kalbfus, the board of commissioners ordered a shipment of 100 more elk (20 male and 80 female,[102] all yearlings or two-year-olds[103]). In addition, Yellowstone made shipments of elk to South Carolina, New York, Missouri, New Mexico, Montana, Idaho, South Dakota, Minnesota, Michigan, Wisconsin, Colorado, Utah, Arizona and Washington that year—totaling 375 redistributed animals.[104]

However, the Pennsylvania shipment would end up being delayed a year due to a foot and mouth disease epidemic spreading among the elk

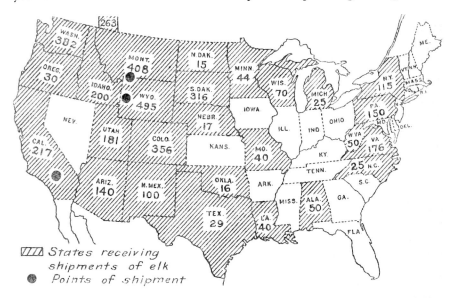

A map published by the U.S. Department of Agriculture illustrating the distribution of elk from 1912 to 1922. *1922.*

in Yellowstone. The outbreak subsided after a year, and the new elk started their journey to Pennsylvania on February 5, 1915, once again under the direction of Howard Eaton,[105] who was responsible for the capture of the initial fifty elk.[106] The new shipment of elk were released in state game lands and refuges in six counties: Cameron, Carbon, Potter, Forest, Blair and Monroe.[107] This cluster of elk, like the last, arrived healthy and unharmed and were able to sustain themselves in the north-central Pennsylvania region. Pennsylvania's elk herd was on track to reestablish itself as one of the largest in the country.

Over the course of the next few years, smaller acquisitions of elk were made by the game commission. In 1918, approximately a dozen elk were donated by an Altoona businessman. In 1924, another six elk were purchased from Wind Cave Game Preserve in South Dakota, and two years later another four elk were purchased.[108] Like most purchases from the Pennsylvania Game Commission, the money used to acquire these elk came from the sale of yearly hunting licenses. These smaller purchases were used to bolster the elk herd's population. Many people in Pennsylvania wanted to see the elk herd thrive, and as a result, private citizens were assisting the game commission in their conservation efforts.

However, farmers were adamantly against the reintroduction of the elk. The species posed a threat to their crops and, as a result, their livelihoods. One of the commissioners who served during the reintegration of the elk, John Phillips, commented on the level of destruction the elk were capable of:

> *When farmers complained, we went into Centre County and found where a band of elk had been raiding a cornfield at night and had destroyed every ear in the field by biting about two inches off the end. They seemed to like the silk.*[109]

As a result, many farmers were forced to take action, with or without the help of the game commission. Many elk were shot for crop damage as a result. Kalbfus believed that farmers were entitled to some form of compensation for their losses, but legislation that would grant crop damage complaints a monetary amount was destined to fail. At the time, lawmakers believed that anyone could submit a claim for crop damage, overexaggerate the damage and leech funds from the government. Therefore, in absence of any laws, the game commission opted to not legally prosecute anyone who shot an elk for crop damage. The farmer could harvest the elk and rid the land of a local nuisance.

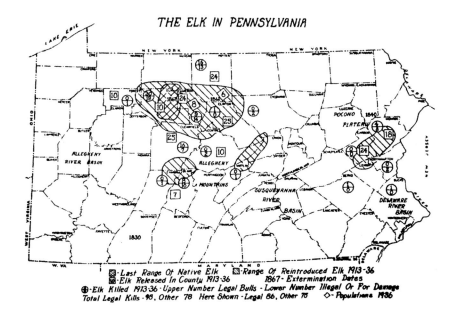

According to this map by the Pennsylvania Game Commission, only fourteen elk were alive by 1936. Cameron County: eight, Potter County: six.

While the elk herd was able to survive, they still faced their fair share of challenges. The 1910s were a difficult time for wildlife in the state. A chestnut blight was running rampant, and as a result, a major source of food for deer, elk, turkeys and many other animals was threatened. Because of the blight, the Pennsylvania Game Commission felt it was necessary to feed much of the wildlife in the affected areas by depositing shipments of hay and clear-cutting forests, which would create natural browsing habitats. This would be just one of the obstacles that the newly arrived elk herd would have to face.[110]

Out of the initial elk shipments to Pennsylvania, none of the elk that were purchased were ever shipped or brought to Elk County, the modern-day home of the herd. Throughout the early twentieth century, the elk acted true to their nature and wandered away from their release sites. It is unclear when exactly the elk first arrived near Benezette and the rest of southeastern Elk County, but eventually they would establish it as a main base of their population.

One of the reasons the elk may have been attracted to the area is because of the terrain. Areas in or around Medix Run, Dents Run and Hicks Run had all been heavily clear-cut during the late nineteenth and early twentieth centuries. By the middle of the twentieth century, the area had started to regrow and, in its early stages, provided great browsing habitats for the elk to live and prosper.

Elk were not the only species that the Pennsylvania Game Commission brought back to the state during this period. In 1915, the commission purchased one thousand ringneck pheasants, which were released in southern and central counties in the state. A year later, the state started a pheasant hatching program in hopes to reestablish the once extinct population. Kalbfus was incredibly pessimistic about the future of these newly introduced birds into the area. In his 1917 report, he wrote:

> *I am more than ever satisfied that the ringneck pheasant is strictly a ground feeder; that it is not a budder, and must be artificially fed when snow covers the ground, or they will just as surely starve as do chickens or tame pigeons under like conditions, and for these reasons can never become a part of the fauna of this commonwealth.* [111]

Soon, however, Kalbfus would be proven wrong, but he would never live to see the successes of the ringneck program. Sadly in 1919, Kalbfus was killed in a train wreck while seeing to his duties as the head of the game commission. He was considered by many to be the father of Pennsylvania conservation and the original leader of the Pennsylvania Game Commission. He was replaced by Seth Gordon, who worked directly under Kalbfus during the last six years of his life. The new executive director of the Pennsylvania Game Commission wrote in his annual report that the ringneck program started by Kalbfus was achieving some success:

> *We received many authentic reports last spring that these birds had positively lived through our severe winter without any assistance. This is very gratifying because before ringnecks were stocked by the commonwealth all the information available indicated that ringnecks could not live for any length of time in Pennsylvania should the ground be covered with ice and snow.* [112]

Another successful reintroduction effort during this time dealt with the once extinct beaver population. John Bennett, the first settler of Bennetts Valley and an expert trapper, reported many beaver dams spanning from Caledonia to Kersey. Eventually, the state's population went extinct, but because of a new effort beavers would once again have a chance at survival.

The initiative, however, was not led by the Pennsylvania Game Commission but instead by two sportsmen who, in 1917, brought a pair of Wisconsin beavers to Cameron County. Soon this pair reproduced and would help reestablish the beaver's population in Pennsylvania. Two years later, the game commission purchased more beavers from Canada and New York, further bolstering the population.[113]

Not every species that the Pennsylvania Game Commission tried to reestablish was a success. Between 1915 and 1918, multiple attempts were made to bring back the quail population. Every one of them failed miserably. Many birds died during shipment, and those that arrived in Pennsylvania did not survive for very long.[114]

While there were some failures along the way, this era marked a new beginning for the Pennsylvania Game Commission. For the first time, the organization was committed to public land management and species reintroduction; previously, the commission solely operated by imposing bag limits, hunting seasons and vermin control.

Even though many great strides were made by the Pennsylvania Game Commission, some antiquated practices were still considered mainstream. In 1913, the State of Pennsylvania enacted bounties on bobcats, foxes, mink, weasels, great horned owls, goshawks and sharp-shinned hawks. The program was established for a few purposes. Firstly, these species needed to be hunted down in order for state refuges to give proper sanctuary for endangered species. Secondly, by eliminating a vast amount of these predatory species from Pennsylvania's landscape, the populations of wild game and other animals would increase throughout the state.

In the same manner that citizens abused and manipulated the Scalp Act of 1883, so too did many Pennsylvania residents take advantage of this system. While Kalbfus was alive, he claimed there were people purchasing weasel skins for eight cents (about two dollars today) in one state who would bring them to Pennsylvania and sell them for two dollars (about fifty today). Kalbfus described the exaggerated claims in the following manner:

> *In one county claims were presented by a man living in another county, this man swearing that he had killed 102 goshawks in four days during the summertime in that county, when at that time there was not one live goshawk in a wild state in this commonwealth. Prior to the passage of this act, no one could, under any condition of circumstances, have made me believe that there were so many men in Pennsylvania willing to commit perjury for a dollar.*[115]

Apparently Kalbfus forgot all about the manipulation that occurred in the 1880s, and Pennsylvania once again paid the price, literally. Upon the conclusion of an investigation into fraudulent claims, it was discovered that the state paid out over $75,000 in improper situations. Over a dozen officials who falsified claims were jailed, and many more claimants were punished. In the defense of the Pennsylvania Game Commission, it was vehemently opposed to this legislature from the beginning, as outlined through the motive not to enact laws to reimburse crop damage claimants.[116]

While there were still many issues that the commission needed to work out, by 1923, Pennsylvania's elk herd was doing well. In fact, it was doing well enough that the commission decided it would be prudent to allow the first official elk hunt. Thirty lucky hunters were awarded tags that year: fifteen allotted for bulls and the rest for cows. In that first year, twenty-three animals were harvested out of those thirty tags. In a 1969 edition of the *Pennsylvania Game News*, Clinton Heller provided an account of when he took part in that inaugural hunt:

We entered the heavily timbered ridge near Devil's Hole in the Mt. Pocono section....A short distance in the timber I saw a herd of elk feeding. I observed them closely, counted them, and picked the one I intended to try for. That bull was the last in line and had the best looking rack. He was standing broadside at not more than 75 yards when I fired. I felt pretty certain about that shot....To my surprise he never flinched. I took very careful aim next and shot with the same results. I fired three shots at that standing bull—a persistent target. The rest of the herd had ran at the first shot. After the third this bull started to go. I fired again and apparently missed. I fired once more and thought I missed again. It ran about 25 yards, stopped turned about to race my way. I looked him over and decided it was not worth shooting any more, although I carried more cartridges in the magazine. I started walking toward the bull. I continued until I was but seven or eight yards from him, then I had looked him over.

I had lost faith in that 32 Special after the first couple of shots. Then, when I stopped walking towards the bull I noticed large streams of blood running down his shoulder. I knew then that the little Marlin wasn't forgotten and my confidence returned a dredfold. I stood there facing the bull, knowing I could down him instantly with a head shot, but certain I need not damage the rack which I wanted for a mount. I decided it was only a matter of a little time until he would bleed out. He did collapse but lay down easily and expired without a struggle. On examination, I found four bullet holes in the chest that could be covered with a tea saucer.[117]

The commission was pleased with the results of the hunt, so it continued annually. The most prosperous year was in 1927, when the total was twenty-six. However, in 1931, the last year for elk hunts in the twentieth century, only one was harvested. During the nine years of active hunting, ninety-eight elk in total were legally harvested, and out of a fear of once again overhunting the animal to extinction, elk hunting in the state was abolished.

At the conclusion of the 1931 hunting season, it was estimated that fewer than fifty elk remained. The *Jeffersonian-Democrat*, a small newspaper operating out of Brookville, credited the statewide closure of the elk hunting season with the illegal harvesting of elk. Allegedly there were twenty elk illegally killed in 1931.[118] While the figure of twenty elk seems within the realm of possibility, the *Bradford Evening Star* asserted that approximately two hundred elk were harvested illegally in the same year.[119] The *Bradford Evening Star*'s report was a gross overestimate. If two hundred elk were removed from the herd, then the elk would have been extinct again. What it does show is that illegal harvests were happening frequently and were generally known and accepted.

Elk were not the only animals to struggle during the 1920s. The population of young deer were threatened due to successive changes in the state's forests. For the beginning of the century, much of the state's forests were composed of sapling thickets, which provided great browsing habitat for deer and elk. However, these areas eventually matured into more developed pole timber areas. Pole timber forests provide little food for browsing animals because much of the food is higher off the ground and out of reach.

Within Clearfield County in a four-township area, game wardens had counted approximately two hundred dead fawns. Those same wardens estimated that in one year one thousand fawns died from starvation. In 1925, the Pennsylvania Game Commission invited Vernon Bailey, a chief field naturalist with the U.S. Biological Survey, to tour the north-central counties of Pennsylvania and examine the forest succession problems. Bailey's report to the game commission provided a dark conclusion for some of Pennsylvania's younger wildlife:

> *In places where the whole slope is grazed to a height of six feet from the ground, fawns and yearlings can not reach to the lowest branches of the trees and are thus deprived of the best food. The low shrubbery is usually closely cropped or exhausted before the higher levels are reached by the larger deer. This apparently is the cause of the recent loss of large numbers of last year's fawns.*[120]

The game commission's conclusion to Bailey's report was that the deer were overpopulated. Pennsylvania's deer problem was becoming eerily similar to Jackson Hole's starving elk problem. The commission's solution was to establish a doe hunting season in order to curb the rapidly growing population. Ross Leffler, the board's president, proclaimed that "Pennsylvania is facing a new type of conservation at the present time, inasmuch as it is necessary in 1928 to kill to conserve."[121]

Due to elk's enormous stature compared to deer, they were less affected by the lack of food created by forest succession. They were taller and able to reach better-quality food in general. Regardless, the natural landscape of Pennsylvania was evolving, and with an elk population facing extinction yet again from overhunting, a change in hunting culture needed to be made.

Perhaps the Great Depression was another reason for the increase in illegal elk killings. Rather than relying on the purchase of food from grocery stores, many people found it more economically viable to hunt game for subsistence instead. According to the game commission, lawlessness was spreading out of control. Poverty-stricken residents were hunting game out of season without purchasing a license and in excess of bag limits. The commission reported that during the winter of 1930–31, game wardens issued fines in a record amount of $96,251.[122]

In 1931, Earnest E. Harwood, the executive director of the Pennsylvania Game Commission at the time, issued a warning to those committing wildlife crimes due to the Great Depression:

> *Unemployment and business conditions touched such a low ebb in the winter of 1931–32 that to have inflicted the full penalties of Game Law upon offenders would have only increased the suffering of their wives and children.*[123]

Harwood and the rest of the game commission were taking a strict approach on conservation. America was in its worst economic state in the twentieth century, and leading conservationists were not about to let residents justify lawlessness because of it.

Perhaps the no-nonsense approach during this period was a byproduct of the social status of the leaders of the commission. It was difficult for the wealthy businessmen and doctors who ran the commission to connect with the vast majority of residents. As a result, it would be even more arduous to enact effective game laws that everyone would follow. Conversely, it was surely possible that the leaders of the commission did understand their constituency but decided that it would be more beneficial to protect and

White-tailed deer side by side with Pennsylvania elk. *Ronald J. Saffer, 2006.*

conserve Pennsylvania's wildlife than to allow decades of conservation work put to waste.

Although policies to prevent overhunting were being strictly enforced, that did not mean bounties were less restricted. In fact, they still existed on raptors and other predatory species throughout the Great Depression. In the late 1920s, a bobcat bounty paid $15; a goshawk, $5; and a gray fox, $4. Many unemployed people looked to this policy as a means to support their families. During the first five years of the Great Depression, Pennsylvania paid out over $520,000 in bounty claims.[124]

However, the governor of Pennsylvania at the time, Gifford Pinchot, aligned himself with raptor preservationists by calling for an end to the bounties. The Pennsylvania Game Commission believed that the public was not ready for an end to the policy and pushed back against the governor's wishes.

Aldo Leopold, a pioneer of American conservation, spoke against bounties to the American Game Association's policy committee in 1932, which underscored the need for new policies to be enacted.

> *We submit that game officials often resort to indiscriminate predator control before food or cover improvement has even been given a fair trial. As a rule, the latter are much more promising as a means of building a game supply.*[125]

The main goal of the bounty policy was to rebuild the game supply in Pennsylvania, so if other measures were proven to be more effective, perhaps it was worth listening to. It would take a few years for the Pennsylvania Game Commission to heed Leopold's advice, when Richard Gerstell denounced the practice. Gerstell was one of the game commission's first full-time wildlife researchers, and he believed that the bobcat population was on the verge of extinction. His research resulted in the bobcat bounty being rescinded in 1937. Additionally, the other bounties on goshawks and weasels would be severely cut in order for the practice to be less profitable. Interestingly enough, the bounties did allow many game animals to rebuild their populations like the white-tailed deer and other smaller mammals. In addition, the removal of Pennsylvania's native predatory species allowed for other animals to take their place. Coyotes began to migrate to Pennsylvania and establish themselves as a new predatory threat. This further demonstrated the general ineffectiveness of predatory bounties.[126]

By 1936, the elk population was struggling to survive. The Pennsylvania Game Commission claimed that only fourteen elk remained alive.[127] Whether or not an elk herd could be maintained over a long period of time was still

American Elk by American artist William Jacob Hays Sr. *1865.*

yet to be determined. If the Pennsylvania elk population could sustain itself, it would be a direct reflection on the environmental makeup and protection of the state. During the early twentieth century, the coal mining industry was starting to flourish and dominate. The environmental effects that resulted from this enterprise would prove costly to the ecology of the surrounding areas and become a massive challenge that would limit the growth of Pennsylvania's elk herd.

From the perspective of the Pennsylvania Game Commission, the process of enacting laws and measures to ensure the successful growth of elk and other species was an arduous one. In 1937, Executive Director Seth Gordon lamented the precarious balancing act he had to maintain:

> *The wildlife administrator—and I speak as one—functions as best he can in the middle of the hubbub. He's in a position not unlike that of the varsity football coach surrounded by alumni. If there's a scarcity of game, he's condemned. And if he produces too much he's liable to be crucified. All too often the sensible management that would provide the ideal, well-rounded conservation program is balked by misunderstanding. Mere protection, and more and more restocking, I can show, will not insure an abundance of wildlife.*[128]

95

Time only proved Gordon right. Over the next few decades of the twentieth century, it became evident that it took more than the Pennsylvania Game Commission and its efforts to ensure an abundance of wildlife in the state. The cooperation of citizens and private groups was vital for Pennsylvania to take the necessary steps to reclaim its once magnificent wilderness.

A bull elk shedding the velvet from its antlers. *Willard Hill, 2022.*

A bull elk, nicknamed "Fred," seen bugling. *Willard Hill, 2005.*

A bull elk creeps through the dandelions. *T Dorsey Imagery, 2016.*

A family of elk gathered near a stream. *T Dorsey Imagery, 2016.*

Two bull elk fighting during the rut. *T Dorsey Imagery, 2017.*

A bull elk bugling on the edge of the forest. *Bob Traveny, 1990s.*

A bull elk crossing a stream. *T Dorsey Imagery, 2017.*

A bull elk enjoys dinner as the sun sets. *T Dorsey Imagery, 2012.*

Two bull elk preparing to fight. *Willard Hill, 2022.*

Bulls are not always fighting. When the rut has concluded, those that have not won control over a harem of cows form bastard groups until the next year. *T Dorsey Imagery, 2017.*

Above: The Battle of the Bennetts Branch. *David Anderson, 2015.*

Left: A young cow looking for food. *David Anderson.*

Above: A bugling bull in the fall fog. *David Anderson, 2012.*

Right: Hiding among the forest. *David Anderson.*

Limpy the lover showing raw and true emotion. *David Anderson, 2014.*

Patrolling the fields during the sunset. *David Anderson, 2016.*

Watching over my three sons. *David Anderson, 2013.*

Two elk watch over a young doe. *Bob Traveny, 1990s.*

This cow has piebaldism, a condition characterized by the absence of cells called melanocytes in certain areas of the skin and hair. *Ronald J. Saffer.*

A bull leading his herd of cows. *Ronald J. Saffer.*

Thousands of years ago, elk had ivory tusks, and hissing exposed them to warn potential enemies. *Ronald J. Saffer.*

A fight breaks out between two bull elk in a stream. *Ronald J. Saffer.*

A bugling bull elk with his family. *Ronald J. Saffer.*

A mother tending to her calf. *Ronald J. Saffer.*

Two bull elk fight in a clearing. *Ronald J. Saffer.*

These two bull elk have yet to shed the velvet from their antlers. *Ronald J. Saffer.*

Above: A cow crosses a stream. *Ronald J. Saffer*.

Left: A bull elk walking through a clearing in the forest. *Ronald J. Saffer*.

Above: Birds require vast forests for habitat and food. With more sustainable forestry practices, the red-bellied woodpecker and many other birds thrive in the state today. *Willard Hill, 2020.*

Right: The great horned owl was once nearly eradicated from the state, but more ethical hunting practices have allowed them to survive. *Willard Hill, 2011.*

Once hunted for bounties, foxes are an important component of Pennsylvania's ecosystem. *Willard Hill, 2021.*

A pack of doe gather during a winter snowfall. *Willard Hill, 2016.*

4

KING COAL

$\mathcal{W}$hile lumber was one of Pennsylvania's most abundant natural resources aboveground, underneath the surface lay massive veins of bituminous and anthracite coal. Before any serious endeavors were made to extract the mineral from Pennsylvania, Philip Tome recognized just how prolific it was.

> *On the north branch of the Kenzua I have seen indications of stone-coal and have no doubt that there are large deposits of it in that vicinity, as well as around the head of Willow Creek.*[129]

What Tome discovered was more than likely a form of bituminous coal. According to the U.S. Geological Survey, bituminous coal is "blocky and appears shiny and smooth," but on further inspection, it has "thin, alternating, shiny and dull layers." In the United States, this coal was used for many purposes ranging from electricity generation to steel making because of its high heating properties.[130]

The first mining operations in Pennsylvania came into existence in the beginning of the 1800s and strongly developed throughout the course of the century. According to Andrew Roy, the author of *A History of Coal Miners of the United States* (1907), the Lehigh Coal Mining Company was the first mining company formed in the state, in 1803. The company shipped anthracite coal from the Lehigh Valley region into Philadelphia. This coal did not seem to burn and was labeled as "black rock," ground up and thrown on the sidewalk as gravel. What the Lehigh Coal Mining company

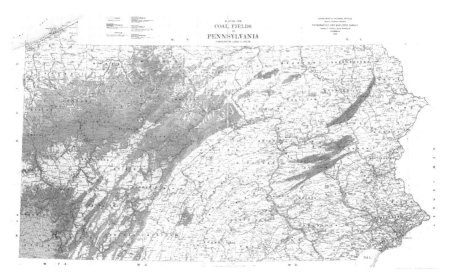

Map of coal fields throughout Pennsylvania. *Pennsylvania Bureau of Topographic and Geologic Survey, 1929.*

was unaware of was that anthracite coal requires an under draft of air to properly burn; this unintuitive procedure most likely lent itself to the reason the Philadelphians could not get it to burn.[131]

While further mining operations were established throughout the state, the introduction of the railroad in the 1840s revolutionized the industry. Roy claimed that within ten years from the first shipments being made by rail, the annual output rose by nearly 6 million tons. In 1853, the state was producing 11 million tons, and in 1873, yearly production was up to 22.88 million tons. Approximately fifty thousand residents were employed as either miners or mine laborers by this time.[132]

When World War I broke out during the late 1910s, the state's now 330,000 miners produced 277 million tons of coal. The resource quickly became the number-one source of fuel for the world, and it would prove to be vital for multiple war efforts in the twentieth century. Worth $705 million at that time (valued at $11.3 billion today), Pennsylvania coal mining was proving to the rest of the country and the world that it was a major player in the industry.[133]

As coal production continued to grow, more miners were needed for the increase in operations. Mining companies throughout the country heavily relied on immigrants to carry that burden. Many people of lower economic classes from southern and eastern Europe were targeted for employment and ultimately came to the beckoning call of the industry.

The Coal Mines by American artist Joseph Pennell depicts a coal mine near Philadelphia. *1916.*

Life as a coal miner was not easy or glamorous. On Friday, October 23, 1936, the front page of the *Daily Press* read, "Father Kept Entombed Son Alive with Breath: Gilbert Bruni Took Heroic Measures to Save His Boy's Life When Latter Was Caught in Mine Cave-In." The article went on to describe the horrific scene that unfolded:

> *A deep human interest story in connection with the rescue of Bruno Bruni, 26, Byrnedale resident, from a mine cave-in at Mine 42 near Byrnedale, has just come to light. When Bruno was caught under 50 to 60 tons of rock Tuesday morning, his father and two young men were in the mines and heard his yell for help. The father rushing to the scene, noted the small quantity of air that could get through the barrier to his boy, ordered the two young men out of the mines to conserve the air supply, extinguished his mine lamp to add to that supply, and then digging a small hole through the rock and dirt with his bare hands breathed his own breath on his then partly conscious son. He kept this up until he saw his boy was reviving, enlarged the hole for further air passage, then going around the barrier started digging in from that side still*

using his bare hands, that today are red and raw, and after 2 hours or more was able to make an opening large enough to drag his son out to safety. It was a ticklish spot for son and father, neither knowing that the next minute might send additional tons of rocks down on them to bury both alive. The young man was taken out of the mine and then brought to the hospital in St. Marys where he is still a patient suffering from a fractured pelvis.[134]

Bruno ended up staying in the hospital for several weeks before being allowed to return home and eventually back to work. He was lucky to be alive, and by extension, so am I. Bruno Bruni is my great-grandfather. When I was a young child, my only memories of Bruno were seeing him sitting in his recliner, breathing from an oxygen machine the size of a fridge. His lungs were permanently damaged from a lifelong career in the mines, and that near-fatal accident did not do him any favors.

Like Bruno, a significant portion of my great-great-grandfathers and great-grandfathers labored in the mines for much of their adult lives. My great-grandfather Dominic Caliari worked his entire life in the mines and, as a result, spent his last years strapped to an oxygen machine and struggling to breathe. A lifetime in the Pennsylvania mines severely damaged their lungs to the extent that they were unable to breathe on their own. They were not alone.

The coal miners of the twentieth century knew and understood the dangers associated with the profession. However, many needed jobs, and the mines were hiring. Van Wagner, former coal miner, folk singer and current high school biology teacher in the Pennsylvania Wilds, described a common motivation for these miners in his 2002 song "Bootleg Miner." In the song, Wagner tells the story of an old, weathered man, who has coal gray hands and a deep scar across his left eye. The man was a coal miner and lived an unimaginably brutal life. Providing for one's family was a matter of life or death. The miner embodied these sentiments as Wagner describes the miner's life story:

Shamokin, Pennsylvania, the Great Depression had come around.
There was nothing great about it pickin' coal underground.
And I had a stick of powder go off premature.
I was a bootleg coal miner years before the war.
So take me down, underground, or take me down below.
Gonna boil up the buggy for its time to shoot some coal.
When your family gets hungry you'll do anything for work.
I carved out a livin' from the Pennsylvania dirt.[135]

The sentiment that the old man explains was one that embodied the spirit of many Pennsylvanians and immigrants who were desperate and needed stability for their families. His generation was willing to do anything, sacrificing their health and life just so their immediate families and posterity could lead better lives.

From the late 1870s to the early 1950s, coal was the number-one source of fuel and energy across the entire United States. The moniker "King Coal" became widely used to showcase the reliance the country had on the resource, and Pennsylvania was primed to be a dominant supplier for the nation. By the start of World War II, the demand for coal had reached its highest point, and much of the supply was coming from Pennsylvania.

Visually speaking, coal mining reshaped the entire state. Areas were clear-cut for the expansive mining operations. Vast seas of company homes were erected around the mines in order to house the workers. Once the mines were in full operation, piles of waste and sludge could be seen throughout the landscape. The elk, deer, birds and countless other species were among the most affected. Their habitats were invaded and transformed into inhospitable locales. Unfortunately, the environmental health effects imposed by the industry would not be addressed for some time.

A principal coal mining operation in the state rested in north-central Pennsylvania in Bennetts Valley. Many of these towns were built on the success of the lumber industry in the previous century. The Pittsburg, Shawmut and Northern Railroad (PS&N) company came to be the leading producer of coal in the area. In 1909, a rail line that ran from Wayland, New York, to Brockport, Pennsylvania, was completed and subsequently connected the coal mining industry of the Valley to the Great Lakes region and the Eastern Seaboard.[136] The range of the new railroad was far reaching, and this was made known early on by the PS&N. Before the line was built, the PS&N gave the following description of how wide ranging of an effect the railroad would have from a preliminary offering contract from 1899:

> The Pittsburg, Shawmut and Northern Railroad is a consolidation and extension of several lines in western Pennsylvania and New York, which, by the construction of connecting lines, forms the shortest and most direct route from the bituminous coal fields to New England and the Lake markets. The new road comprises the Buffalo, St. Marys and Southwestern Railroad, the Clermont, Mt. Jewett and Northern Railroad, the Clarion River Railroad, and the Central New York and

Western Railroad, with connections forming a line 230 miles in length, from the Shawmut coal fields in Elk County, Penn., via St. Marys, Smethport, Olean, Angelica, and Hornellsville to Wayland N.Y.[137]

Within the same preliminary offering, the PS&N claimed that the yearly production of the Shawmut mines in the past few years had been about 600,000 tons and that "new and improved electrical machinery has been ordered, much of which is already in place, which will ensure an output of approximately one million tons the present year, and, say, one million and a half tons the next year."[138]

The PS&N never did reach that goal of 1.5 million tons annually. However, at its peak, throughout World War II, the PS&N was able to produce approximately 1 million tons of coal annually in the Valley from two main mines and a few smaller operations. Per day, the Tyler mine produced 500 tons, with smaller mines contributing 400 tons; the Cardiff mine, which is, at present, a mere ghost town, produced 1,300 tons; and mines in Force added 300 tons.[139] All of these operations were owned and controlled by the PS&N, which profited mightily from operations in the Valley.

While not owned by the PS&N, coke ovens throughout the Valley were profitable industries. The largest of which, the ovens in Tyler, employed up to six hundred people at its peak. The foundations of these structures can still be seen today.

Entrance at the Tyler coke ovens. *Mt. Zion Historical Society.*

In addition to providing jobs to the area, the PS&N established a railroad, which allowed for commodities and luxury items to be easily imported. General merchandise, forest products, sewer pipe, tile, oil products, farm produce, beer and many more goods were transported over the lines. The railroads provided what seemed like foreign luxuries to the small communities. Donald Chiappelli, a lifelong resident, local historian of the Bennetts Valley area, and my grandfather, described the presence of the 1940s railroads in the following firsthand account:

> *Weedville was a busy, independent town then, with many stores and its own high school. Look across the highway from my father's grocery store, there on Route 555, and follow down along Kersey Run. You'll see that Weedville was a town of railroads. Three of them. On the south side of the Bennetts Branch ran two rail lines. The farther one was the great Pennsylvania railroad, "The Pennsy." It was the big one, the main line, employing a quarter million people and stretching across the Northeast into the Midwest. The Pennsy had a payroll larger than the federal government. It hauled freight and passengers—many, many passengers.*
>
> *The Pennsy was the "high grade" railroad. Its rail ascended westward at a higher elevation than the other interstate railroad that ran through the valley, the B&O, or Baltimore and Ohio. Formerly known as the Baltimore and Susquehanna, the B&O ran on a bed known as the "low grade." The B&O was predominantly a freight line.*[140]

While Chiappelli's claim that the "Pennsy" had a larger payroll than the U.S. government was inaccurate, he was not far off. The Pennsylvania Railroad had the reputation of being the largest publicly owned business in the United States during the early 1900s. Throughout the railroad's prime, the only other organization that had a greater operating budget was, in fact, the U.S. government.[141]

These new railroads built in the Valley significantly expedited the industrialization of the area. Those in charge of the railroads and the mines were able to operate at a much higher level than previously seen. However, the new faster pace at which the mining industry was operating proved to be disastrous to the local wildlife of the area, including the elk herd. Nonetheless, the environmental and wildlife issues were put on the back burner as new forms of commerce arrived and profitability increased.

The Pennsy and the B&O brought commerce to the Valley on a level never before seen by the community. The railroads that went through

A coal train traveling on the Pennsylvania Railroad through Indiana County, Pennsylvania. *Wikimedia Commons, photo taken before 1934.*

Bennetts Valley were a prevalent part of daily life for those who lived there. However, there was a third railroad that ran through the area, one owned by the PS&N. Chiappelli continued in his account by describing the cultural influences that this railroad had on the area:

> *Closest to my father's store was the Shawmut line. Its station and water tower stood where the post office is today. The Shawmut was more of a local affair. It strictly hauled coal from the mines of the valley—with one exception. Every fall, my father purchased a carload of grapes, and the Shawmut delivered that railcar to a siding near his store. Then he sold grapes to people all around the Valley for winemaking. My father arranged railcars of grapes for other communities in the area, too.*[142]

The Valley was predominantly settled by Italian immigrants. The grapes that Louis Chiappelli distributed gave the residents an opportunity to be more in touch with their cultural roots. It gave them a sense of home in a foreign place, for many had emigrated from Italy in search of work. Winemaking was an avenue in which the miners could find joy outside of the hard labors of their work, and the Shawmut was indirectly responsible for providing that.

However, most of the effects that the Shawmut had on the area were not as positive as the freight of grapes. The PS&N was formed under the leadership of John Byrne in 1899, while backed by Boston interests. Six years later, in 1905, the PS&N went bankrupt but continued to operate unabated, hauling out millions of tons of coal for the next forty-two years.[143] During this period—and while operating under complete bankruptcy—the miners employed by the PS&N were reduced to inhumane living conditions while the corporate executives continued to rake in sizable salaries.

The train station and water tower in Weedville. *Courtesy of Mt. Zion Historical Society, photo taken during the 1930s.*

The community of Force, a town on the southern border of Weedville, was the most severely affected mining community as far as living conditions were concerned. The water was heavily polluted from sewage and mining wastes, and the residents lived in poorly maintained company homes.

Eventually, frustration grew, and the miners started to coalesce behind the PS&N's company doctor, Dr. Elizabeth O. Hayes, a Force native. Left with no choice, Dr. Hayes and the leaders of the miners organized walkouts and refused to continue working until the company rectified the "intolerable sanitary conditions."[144]

Since the genesis of the mining village, the roads were dirt, and if there was any rain, they would turn to mud. Historian Marcia Biederman, author of *A Mighty Force*, described the struggles of Dr. Hayes and the inhumane living conditions of Force and specifically provided an account of the dangers inherent with these poor road conditions:

> *The mud-puddle streets nearly took the life of one of* [Dr. Hayes's] *patients when an ambulance, summoned from DuBois, sank down to its fenders. Hayes' car became mired, too, causing a dangerous delay. The community came up with a proposal to pave the road with "red dog," a mining waste product. The rose-colored gravel would cost Shawmut Mining nothing, and the miners offered to contribute the labor in their spare time.*[145]

Though cost-free, Shawmut provided initial resistance to the plan before eventually allowing the miners to gravel the roads with what would normally have been hauled off as waste.

Outhouses decorate the front yard of company mining homes in Force. *Jack Delano, 1940.*

In the aforementioned account, Chiappelli provided a graphic description referencing the new red dog roads. In the following quote, Chiappelli uses "Weedville" as a general term for the Valley, including Force, which is a common occurrence.

> *Weedville was a louder place in those days, with trains whistling through all the time. It was dirtier too, with the steam engines exhausting soot. Sulfur filled the air from the rock dumps where the mines caught fire. That burning coal produced red dog. I can't believe they once used the red dog cinders to gravel the roads. It turned the creeks red and polluted them all the more.*[146]

While the new roads were better than what Force and Weedville had before, they were by no means perfect. The red dog, when rained on, would wash down into the local streams, turning them a reddish orange hue. The creeks were the main source of drinking water for the local wildlife, which did not have any alternatives because nearly all the waterways in the Valley were severely polluted.

The village of Force did not have running water and relied on outhouses for sewage disposal. This too would eventually pollute the local waterways and topsoil of the community. What was even more affected was the drinking wells. The town relied on twenty-one wells and natural springs for drinking, cooking and bathing water; when government officials were sent to evaluate the cleanliness of Force, eleven of the wells as well as many of the springs were found to be polluted, including the spring from which Dr. Hayes gathered drinking water for her practice.

The PS&N claimed that boiling the water would then make it usable for the many families that resided in Force. Dr. Hayes fired back, claiming that "boiling takes care of the sanitation angle, so everything ought to be perfectly alright if you don't mind drinking perfectly sanitary sewage."[147] And perfectly sanitary sewage is what residents of Force were forced to consume. Gathering and boiling water became an all-day job for the women. The elk and local wildlife did not have the benefit of boiled water, so they were left to consume water inundated with mining and human waste.

By this time, the PS&N was bankrupt for nearly forty years, and with that came forty years of neglect toward the coal miners of Force and the surrounding mining towns of Byrnedale, Weedville, Tyler, Cardiff and Hollywood. In an attempt to gain publicity about the terrible living conditions, Dr. Hayes spoke to a Pulitzer Prize–winning journalist, Ray Spriger of the

Byrnedale company homes were just as run-down as those in nearby Force. *Jack Delano, 1940.*

Pittsburgh Post-Gazette. Spriger made a name for himself through his lengthy multi-series columns on previously untold narratives. He believed that the story of Force was another saga that needed to be exposed to the public. He eventually visited Force on multiple occasions and, in doing so, was given a list of demands from Dr. Hayes that she and the coal miners felt they were entitled to.

In August 1945, Spriger published the demands of Dr. Hayes in one of his many articles on the town:

> *We've got our demands ready whenever the company condescends to listen to us. We want pure water piped in from outside. This whole area is contaminated many feet down. We want inside toilets and some method of sewage disposal. The men will install the toilets and pay water rents. We want kitchen and bath water disposed of, other than being run into the streets as at present. We want passable streets. With millions of tons of red dog—mountains of it—a few hundred feet away the company has never hauled a pound of it to take us out of the mud and dust. We want garbage and rubbish removal facilities of some kind. We want the unsightly coal sheds taken out of front yards. In short, we just want to live like other human beings, not like cattle.*[148]

Feeling neglected and treated like second-class citizens, Dr. Hayes and her miner cohort demanded to be brought up to standard, humane living conditions.

It was not Dr. Hayes's responsibility to fight for a clean community, but she did it anyway. The United Mine Workers Association (UMWA) was the national union that represented miners across the country. Led by John L. Lewis, the UMWA had made a name for itself in 1943 when it successfully negotiated new mining contracts for every coal miner in America. Due to the United States' overwhelming reliance on coal for its ongoing efforts in World War II, the government essentially commandeered control of the mining industry in the country, and as a result, this allowed Lewis and the UMWA to negotiate with one entity for nearly every coal miner.

The new contract was born from a lengthy work stoppage and protest across the country. While many World War II historians believed that the outcome of the war was already decided by 1943, a halt to coal production could stymie the Allied war effort. Therefore, any large-scale strike in the country demanded quick and effective action. "The continuance of idleness in the mines will prove a great source of inspiration to Hitler, Mussolini, and company," wrote the *DuBois Courier Express*.[149] Fears that the Axis powers could somehow come back and win World War II were fully manifested when President Franklin D. Roosevelt threatened to send troops to the coal mines, to which Lewis countered, "You can't dig coal with bayonets."[150]

The fear of work stoppages and strikes was far-reaching across the United States. As a result, when one small town in the middle of the Pennsylvania forests refused to work until viable living conditions were established, neither the UMWA nor any aspect of the federal government came to their aid. Instead, Dr. Hayes saw herself as the only force that could defend her friends and neighbors and fight for what nearly every community in the country considered commonplace.

The village of Force was victim to greedy corporations that wanted to milk every cent that they could from the ecosystem of north-central Pennsylvania. In an emotional plea for help to any outside agency, Dr. Hayes asserted that the people of the Valley

deserve something better. If not for ourselves, then for our children....For years my father, and then I, have been counseling these mothers to go to a hospital to bear their children. They're doing that now. We've taught them to adhere religiously to the formulas for feeding that we devise: plenty of orange juice, cod liver oil and other things that modern child care dictates.

Many boys came to work in mines throughout Pennsylvania. This photograph depicts workers from South Pittston. *Lewis Wickes Hine, 1911.*

They're doing that, too. So we mix our carefully worked out baby formulas, not with water, but with dilute urine and fecal matter. Of course we boil it so it's sanitary. But you wouldn't exactly call it palatable baby-fare, now would you?[151]

It was clear to everyone that the living conditions surrounding the coal mining towns were not ideal by any stretch of the imagination. This was underscored by the fact that many of the servicemen from the Valley, who were fighting wars on two fronts across the globe, were refusing to return to their hometown. Dr. Hayes was quoted in an article published by the *Kane Republican* in August 1945 saying that "they can see no reason for fighting for something on foreign soil and then not even having it in their own homes."[152] For as sparsely populated as these towns were, many of the men had still joined the service, as indicated by plaques displayed in the mining towns to honor them.

Dr. Hayes was chiefly responsible for these memorials throughout the Bennetts Valley area. The monuments served to create a sense of community among the residents and the men fighting overseas. "Hayes, who was passionately committed to honoring the local service members," wrote Biederman, "saw a chance to create something clean, lasting, and dignified in this almost comically deteriorating place. The residential section of Force might be called 'the Patch,' but its young men were fighting for an America they'd seen in the movies."[153]

While Dr. Hayes and the residents of Force were fighting to keep a community alive, the Pennsylvania Game Commission's fight for conservation had not been forgotten. In fact, many within the commission were troubled that what they had struggled for over the previous fifty years was in danger of being lost. With much of Pennsylvania's male population going to war, the game commissioners rightfully anticipated a severe drop in license purchases. As a result, a wartime reserve fund was established to fund the conservation efforts that needed to be upheld throughout the war, specifically for maintaining public game lands, supporting wildlife management and paying game wardens to enforce wildlife laws.

At a state sportsmen's club in Wellsboro, a pledge was made by its members. United States Fish and Wildlife director Ira Gabrielson reported that the declaration made was as follows:

> *I pledge my heart and my right hand to my flag and my country. I further pledge myself to help carry out the wildlife conservation program, now in progress, to the end that your boy and my boy, now serving his country, may find the good hunting and fishing he has a right to expect, when he returns to civil life.*[154]

This pledge was successfully upheld. Throughout the war, hunting license sales averaged $600,000 per year, and by the end of the war, the Pennsylvania Game Commission had $1.3 million leftover in reserve funds. It would appear that not even Hitler could get in the way of Pennsylvania's conservationists.

Surprisingly, the Pennsylvania Game Commission prospered throughout the course of World War II. The commission's land management program was progressing well. In less than forty years, the program went from managing a few game preserves to more than one million acres of game lands. However, most men were overseas, and the game commission was now hampered by a lack of manpower. The game commission needed help, and the remaining sportsmen throughout the state were willing to pitch in. Joe Kosack described the involvement of organized groups and individuals as "helping field personnel feed game in winter, cut browse, build brush piles, and perform other habitat development work." The community involvement seen here signaled one of the first instances of sportsmen taking

A postcard from York, Pennsylvania, of an elk statue. *York News Agency, created between 1930 and 1945.*

a direct approach to conservation in tandem with the Pennsylvania Game Commission. The relationship between the two would prove to be necessary if great strides in protecting Pennsylvania's environment were to continue after the war.[155]

While the lumber industry took a backseat to coal mining during the twentieth century, that did not mean that it was entirely forgotten. In fact, the Pennsylvania Game Commission profited mightily from the sale of timber from their expansive game lands. Guided by ethical practices of forestry, the lumber on these lands was harvested in a manner that would be both profitable for the commission and sustainable for the local wildlife. Applying the principles endorsed by Rothrock and Pinchot, areas were harvested by sections to allow certain patches to remain untouched, while others were entirely harvested. This simultaneously allowed the commission to profit from the lumber while keeping many habitats safe. Seth Gordon, the executive director of the game commission, commented on the habitat improvements created from ethical forestry practices during this time: "Studies by employees, as well as observations by sportsmen, indicate that cuttings which have been made on game lands in the past have materially improved habitat for wildlife."[156] It was apparent that the values of sustainable forestry instilled by Rothrock and Pinchot had survived and were still being promoted nearly fifty years later.

While the Pennsylvania Game Commission's environmental efforts did not lose focus, many mining towns throughout America were still suffering from poor living conditions. Throughout the country, factories were dumping waste into the local waterways, and America's growing population was producing an increasing amount of sewage. Pesticides were becoming more heavily used to kill insects and protect agricultural fields. Combined with poor mining practices, the waterways were polluted all the more. Albert Day, a U.S. Fish and Wildlife Service official, addressed the current state of America's water pollution in a 1947 report:

Pollution of our streams—always bad—became worse during the war. New industrial plants sprang up overnight, and the disposal of their wastes was given little consideration. Plants using new manufacturing processes dumped new types of waste into the streams, and time did not permit adequate study to devise safe disposal methods. War housing communities sprang up overnight, and the treatment of domestic sewage lagged because of shortages of critical materials. We slipped a long way in the fight to correct a pollution situation that was already growing worse instead of better.[157]

About a decade before Day's report of pollution in the country and Dr. Hayes's fight against the PS&N, the Pennsylvania legislature passed the Clean Streams Act of 1937. Section 4 of the new law firmly declared its motivations:

(1) Clean, unpolluted streams are absolutely essential if Pennsylvania is to attract new manufacturing industries and to develop Pennsylvania's full share of the tourist industry;

(2) Clean, unpolluted water is absolutely essential if Pennsylvanians are to have adequate out of door recreational facilities in the decades ahead;

(3) It is the objective of the Clean Streams Law not only to prevent further pollution of the waters of the Commonwealth, but also to reclaim and restore to a clean, unpolluted condition every stream in Pennsylvania that is presently polluted.

(4) The prevention and elimination of water pollution is recognized as being directly related to the economic future of the Commonwealth.[158]

The law made appeals to two important sides of the argument. First off, new businesses would not move to Pennsylvania if the streams were severely polluted and the landscape was in ruins; the attraction of new businesses was vital for the future of the state. Secondly, clean streams are needed to keep Pennsylvanians in Pennsylvania. If the natural landscape of Pennsylvania loses its beauty, then it loses its greatest natural resource in the pursuit of short-term economic gains.

The Clean Streams Act was met with much praise from the public and the Pennsylvania Game Commission. The *Pennsylvania Game News*, a publication controlled by the commission, published an editorial supporting the legislation:

> *If ever a piece of legislation for the benefit of the whole people merited enactment this one does. Pure streams insure good water for domestic and industrial uses, better health and more outdoor recreation. Polluted, unsanitary streams are the signposts of decay, death, and desolation. If we continue to tolerate them by not supporting the bill in question we shall justly deserve the reward we shall ultimately reap.*[159]

As would be expected, many industries did not initially comply with the Clean Streams Act. The waterways had already been polluted for some time when the 1937 legislation was signed into law, and it was a last-ditch effort to mandate a remedy. Defiantly, the PS&N continued to pollute the streams around Force and their other mines. Ultimately, the residents of Bennetts Valley paid the price.

After Dr. Hayes garnered publicity for the living conditions in Force, many people began to take notice of similar abuse in their own communities. In an article published by the *Pittsburgh Post-Gazette* in August 1945, an unnamed author shared frustrations about the lack of care shown toward mining communities.

> *There are still a few mining companies which believe that private enterprise means the right to do what you damn please wherever you have title to a piece of land. You can strip mine it and leave an eye-sore for others to worry about. You can maintain a stinking gob pile, the fumes of which ruin crops and forests within a radius of ten or twenty miles. Or you can run a rural slum.*[160]

The rural slum that the author referred to is not the village of Force but the now common, run-down and neglected mining towns throughout

Pennsylvania and many other states due to pollution from greedy, careless corporations. The ignorant leaders of the mining companies in Pennsylvania did not live anywhere near their operations. Therefore, they were never subject to the poor living conditions surrounding these communities.

The PS&N executive in charge of Force resided in New York, while many of the initial founders of the company were from Boston. It was impossible for the leaders to empathize with these communities because they viewed the laborers of Force as a commodity that earned the company revenue. The heads of the PS&N were out for themselves, and themselves only. Little regulation had existed on mining operations, and companies encouraged exploitation when it could help increase profit, all to the displeasure and punishment of the coal miner.

The hardships that the residents of Force were faced with strengthened the community. The shared trauma was the kindling that Dr. Hayes needed to light the fire against the PS&N. Forged through constant neglect by the mine operators, the community of Force was empowered to fight for the lives of its residents.

The unnamed author from the *Pittsburgh Post-Gazette* also pointed out an important issue that had been all but forgotten in the war for public health: the well-being of the local environment. If the streams and underground wells were polluted with sewage, making it unsanitary for humans to drink, then it was not sanitary for any other living creature. The red dog discolored the creeks, and poor mining practices inundated them with sulfur and other metals. An ecosystem cannot be expected to thrive if these are the conditions imposed on it. At least the people of Force had drinking access to sanitarily boiled sewage.

The struggling elk population had to drink whatever water was available to them. Although the reintroduced elk herd was originally placed in counties throughout north-central Pennsylvania, they had begun to migrate to areas in southeastern Elk County, more specifically Force, Weedville, Caledonia and Benezette—all of which reside on the Bennetts Branch of the Sinnemahoning River. Mine pollution severely affected this body of water, which would prove harmful to the surrounding wildlife for years to come. In fact, the water became devoid of all aquatic life. Native species of trout and eel were lost forever. The streams where President Grant once vacationed were entirely unfishable, and the water was left undrinkable. According to the Pennsylvania Game Commission's website, the population of the elk herd in 1945 was anywhere between 20 and 30, far smaller from the initial 177 imported during the 1910s.[161] The neglected habitat and unclean water

Cow and Calf Elk by American artist, naturalist and wildlife biologist Olaus Murie. *Early 1930s.*

proved to be major limiting factors in the path to restoring Pennsylvania's once mighty elk herd.

Additionally, overhunting practices rebounded on the conclusion of World War II. As soldiers returned home and into the woods to hunt, the Pennsylvania Game Commission witnessed an unprecedented rise in wildlife lawlessness. In the notes of a 1946 commission meeting, the overall discontent toward the current state of affairs was addressed:

> *The general conduct of the hunters afield during the 1946 season was unsatisfactory, and in a number of regions there was appalling evidence of lawlessness and meat-hungry greediness. This was especially noticeable during the deer season, the percentage of illegal kills being much higher than normal. Total penalties collected for the fiscal year will apparently be $115,000 to $120,000, as against a normal of $50,000 to $60,000. The previous high was $96,000 collected in 1931.*[162]

The disregard for established game practices was not localized to Pennsylvania. Waves of game-related crime were seen throughout the United States and Canada. Attorney S. Dale Furst Jr. of the Pennsylvania

Federation of Sportsmen's Clubs stated that wildlife-related prosecutions were up more than 80 percent.

Joe Kosack provided multiple explanations that illustrated this uptick in insolence. One notion was that the returning servicemen had adopted a "school's out" approach to wildlife. After experiencing extensive trauma during the war, many disregarded "irrelevant" game laws because they risked their lives for America and felt the laws did not apply to them. Other scholars contended that an increase in the cost of living postwar forced many to break the law in order to provide for their family. Many more believed that the spike was temporary and would eventually subside. The Pennsylvania Game Commission needed to make a shift in its public policy if it were to convince the state's outdoorsmen to stick to sustainable conservation practices.

As the state game commission was dealing with legal problems, so were Dr. Hayes and the residents of Force. The work protests had become national news across the country, with Dr. Hayes at the forefront. Eventually, a cry for help landed in President Truman's office. Sending a message to him was akin to locating a black cat in a coal cellar, but a presidential secretary identified the plea and forwarded it to the Department of Justice to be handled by the criminal division.[163]

The management of the PS&N came under great scrutiny from federal prosecutors. Throughout the course of the investigation, it was uncovered that no accurate accounting records were kept from 1942 to 1945, and that the company was suffering from a crippling amount of debt.

Now that the company's skeletons were coming out of the closet, the PS&N was losing any semblance of public trust. Any trust that may have remained after the investigation was lost when the company's law enforcement officer and mine foreman raided Dr. Hayes's house.

Public police forces were not common in many areas, especially rural coal mining towns like Force. As a result, the PS&N had multiple private investigators on payroll that would act as local law enforcement. This practice was quite common throughout the country, and the PS&N was not any different. Francis Erich was the man the PS&N charged with keeping the peace in Force. However, by this time, coal mining police had been outlawed at the federal level, but since the PS&N was also a railroad company, Erich acted as a railroad cop.

At this point, the PS&N hired a new company doctor to replace Dr. Hayes, and therefore, the company needed her to vacate her house. The house that she grew up in, that her father practiced medicine in as well, was owned by the PS&N; it was a company home, slightly nicer than the company houses that the coal miners resided in. The PS&N had every right to evict Dr. Hayes, but the manner in which they did was forceful and undermined basic lawfulness. Marcia Biederman described the events in the following manner:

> *On November 13, Erich drove to Force with an eviction notice for Hayes....Humiliated in the press and facing possible financial ruin, Dickson (the leader of the PS&N) was determined to fight to the last ditch. Shawmut would kick Hayes out of her company-owned office and install the new doctor. Erich, scouting for Hayes so he could hand-deliver his letter, couldn't have been pleased that it was 10:00 p.m. when he finally encountered her.*[164]

"We respectfully request that you arrange to vacate these offices in this building and on these premises before the close of the week ending November seventeenth." On four days' notice, Dr. Hayes was expected to completely vacate her childhood home. Five-day eviction notices were not uncommon, but those were for tenants behind on their rent. Dr. Hayes's rent was paid on time, in full, every month. Given the letter's preposterous nature, Dr. Hayes did not take it seriously.

Dr. Hayes was serving house calls and tending to the wellness of the Force residents when five men broke into her home that Saturday. When she came home that day around 2:30 p.m., she witnessed men moving furniture and medical supplies from her house into a moving van. Dr. Hayes furiously approached the men and told them that what they were doing was against the law. David Bell, the mine superintendent and one of the men removing her property, pointed to Francis Erich and said, "He's the law around here."

Now homeless, Dr. Hayes was lucky enough to have family in nearby Brockway. Staying with her sister and mother, she continued to fight for the miners, even after having all of her personal possessions and medical supplies stripped from her. Within a week, she had contacted the district attorney of Elk County, Edward Blatt, who filed charges against three of the men involved in the raid of her home.

As the case against Erich, Bell and one other man was underway, the PS&N was also facing a legal battle of its own. A district court in Pittsburgh was conducting a hearing to see if the receiver, John D. Dickson, was to be replaced as the head of the PS&N. The Monday after being evicted from her home, Dr. Hayes testified all day against the PS&N. Three other miners and community leaders—Bill Agosti, Tony Coccimiglio and Joe Shadick— testified in hearings on Tuesday. Coccimiglio described the state of the company homes from the following court testimony:

> *The houses are nothing to brag about. You could swing a cat through the cracks in some of them. Come up sometime, and be sure to stop in and get a smell of our drinking water when we boil it....Dickson was too busy to take three hours off to talk to his own men. Today was the first time I ever saw Dickson.*[165]

For Dr. Hayes and everyone in Force, this hearing needed to achieve more than replacing the current leadership of the PS&N. Serious and effective measures needed to be taken to clean Bennetts Valley. While many news outlets had shown public support for the residents of Force, that did not mean everyone was empathetic. The *Pittsburgh Post-Gazette* was perhaps the most vocal supporter of Dr. Hayes. Ray Spriger had given her a public platform, and the reporter attacked the PS&N at every angle. As a result, some who supported the coal company wrote to the paper, denouncing the newspaper and the miners in the process. In an effort to expose the ignorance of these attacks, the *Pittsburgh Post-Gazette* published one of the letters to the editor written by a John F. Fitzgerald:

> *Your paper simply must stop its present dangerous radicalism. The espousing of the case of the lady doctor and the miners in sewage-infested towns is a case in point. Don't you know that miners are not people, that they are supposed to be just a bit sub-human, not satisfied unless dirty, unshaven, uncontrolled, and on strike?*[166]

While Fitzgerald did not live in or near Force, those living in St. Marys held similar opinions. The town of St. Marys is about a ten-minute drive north of Force, and it was where the headquarters of the PS&N was located. Dickson made sure that the *Pittsburgh Post-Gazette* was not sold in stores in the town, leaving many residents unaware of what was going on in nearby Force. An editorial that was published after the district court's ruling in *The Daily Press* juxtaposed how the residents of Force and St. Marys perceived the PS&N.[167]

> *The local company was depicted as an organization not interested in what might be termed "human welfare," while in St. Marys we know*

A view from the outskirts of a mining town in rural Shenandoah, Pennsylvania. *Sheldon Dick, 1938.*

different. The Pittsburg, Shawmut and Northern Railroad Company was a stable enterprise that paid good wages in most instances....Silence isn't always golden.[168]

Throughout the course of Dr. Hayes's twenty-week protest, a free press was not allowed to exist in St. Marys. Dickson made sure of that. However, every attempt he made to violate the law was made in vain, as the presiding judge ruled in favor of Dr. Hayes and Force. Dickson was to be replaced as the company receiver, and serious efforts to improve the living conditions of Force were mandated.

The Force Hotel is a historic landmark in the Valley. Its longevity allowed it to witness nearly every great event in the history of Bennetts Valley. On November 29, 1945, Dr. Hayes and her cohort of miners were at the Force Hotel waiting to hear the result of the case. When the phone rang, Bill Agosti answered and soon announced to everyone that "Dickson's out!" A reporter present at the Force Hotel described Dr. Hayes's reaction:

Betty started to cry. Vincent (Dr. Hayes' brother who had just come into town that day) was sitting by himself in a corner. "I wish my dad was around," he said. Bill Agosti looked at them both thoughtfully for a moment. "Old Doc Hayes ain't dead," he said.[169]

Other cries were documented as the news was announced. The oldest member of Dr. Hayes's protest, Frank Winkler, yelled out, "Forty years of tyranny shot to hell, we'll have that Boston Tea Party now."[170]

Dr. Hayes received another notch in her win column soon thereafter when Francis Erich, David Bell and a third culprit were convicted of forcible entry when her home was raided. The charge carried a fine of up to $500 and up to one year imprisonment. Although Dickson's henchmen were convicted by a jury, the judge overseeing the case decided to throw out the jury's decision due to the potential bias caused by the PS&N's recently smeared public image. The men were set free of penalty and legal wrongdoing, and the district attorney opted not to appeal the decision. Yet to Dr. Hayes and everyone else, it did not matter; the men were already convicted by public opinion.

Winning the legal battle against Dickson and the PS&N took the willpower of the entire Valley, state and national politicians. Dr. Hayes received national praise and attention, so much that she was featured in

Time magazine.[171] The organization reported the last stages of Dr. Hayes's fight in the following manner:

> *"Pure water should be the first requirement of a community. I think it would pay in the end to clean up. It is economically wise to make a better community," claimed Federal Judge Guy K. Bard. He appointed new receivers, who agreed to fix up the wells and the sewage. The miners were expected to go back to work. Dr. Betty is already on the job.*

Additionally, the legendary country singer Woody Guthrie wrote a song that embodied her fighting spirit, "The Dying Doctor." In a portion of the song, Guthrie chronicled Dr. Hayes's resilience and the abject living conditions of the mining town:

> *With her face so pretty and her smile so sweet.*
> *She walked the coal towns of Force and Byrnedale;*
> *She saw the sewage waters flowing down the street.*
> *She saw the children drink the cankered water,*
> *She saw the chickens fly up on the roof,*
> *She saw the waters overflow the sewers,*
> *And flood their gardens of victory.*
> *She went to the big shots of the Shawmut Company,*
> *She did not beg and she did not plead,*
> *She stood flatfooted and pounded the table,*
> *Sewer pipes and bathrooms are what we need.*[172]

Dr. Hayes had won the first battle in the war for public health in Bennetts Valley and in doing so gave Force national attention, but much work still needed to be done in order to reclaim the lands that had been abused for more than a century.

In 1947, two years after the first walkout began, the PS&N was forced to close and recolonize under the New Shawmut Mining Company with leadership handpicked by the presiding judge. The former company homes in the village of Force that belonged to the PS&N were now owned by the individual miners. The people of the Valley had gained a sense of place and ownership. Bennetts Valley was in the process of being cleaned up, a freer community was growing and there was hope that the elk herd could flourish once again.

Dr. Hayes stood up against the stereotypical embodiment of a corporation from America's Gilded Age. She, and her cohort of miners, would be known as the first group to try to clean up Bennetts Valley. Dr. Hayes wanted the Valley to be much more than a town of miners; she wanted to create a thriving community. One of her initiatives was to establish honor rolls for each of the towns under the PS&N's domain. These honor rolls would memorialize those who fought in the Second World War by listing off their names on a central monument. The villages of Force, Hollywood, Weedville and Penfield all proudly display these honor rolls today.

By giving the miners their own homes and creating community memorials, the efforts of Dr. Hayes united the residents of the Valley for decades to come. All of this was underscored by the continual popularity of Weedville's annual Homecoming Celebration, which occurs every year on Labor Day. The celebration was designed to welcome back everyone who served during World War II. Amusement rides and parades are the hallmarks of the weekend-long celebration; vendors from charitable organizations serve food to all those in attendance; and in most recent years, a three-on-three basketball tournament has brought the homecoming celebration new life.

The most accurate way to describe what this ceremony means to those from the old mining towns is to reiterate conversations that I have with those

Like all wildlife, elk need a clean source of water to prosper and thrive. *David Anderson, 2014.*

Aided by a salt lick and strategic placement of brush, a photographer was able to capture a photograph of this elk near Benezette in the late 1940s. *Mt. Zion Historical Society.*

unfamiliar with the area. Every year I drove from college to come home and celebrate. When I was questioned about why, I responded, "The way you view Christmas is the same way we view Labor Day in the Valley."

If Dr. Hayes was still alive today, there would be no doubt that she would be proud of the community that Bennetts Valley has become. However, it would take many more decades to see the full force of conservation and environmental cleanup take shape, chiefly due to the economic class of those living in the Valley.

Many of the people of Force did not have the economic resources to clean up and take care of the local wildlife. Like my great-grandfathers Bruno Bruni and Dominic Caliari and the subject of Van Wagner's "Bootleg Miner," their number one priority was to provide for their families; everything else was secondary. When the miners received ownership of the company homes, they established permanent residences that would give themselves economic security. The revitalization of the community created an immense sense of belonging, which became the foundation that allowed generational wealth to accrue and remain in the area. Future generations will soon be able to afford to clean up the local environment and dedicate time and resources to its continual improvement. However, with the elk population struggling to survive in the region, the community would need to get rich quickly if it had any chance of keeping whatever was still left of the herd.

5

OPERATION SCARLIFT

*I*n 1971, the Pennsylvania legislature passed an amendment to the state constitution. The new bill secured an additional right for the residents of Pennsylvania, one that should have been inherent since the state's formation under William Penn. Article 1, Section 27 of the Pennsylvania State Constitution reads as follows:

> *The people have a right to clean air, pure water, and to the preservation of the natural, scenic, historic and esthetic value of the environment. Pennsylvania's public natural resources are the common property of all the people, including generations yet to come. As trustee of these resources, the Commonwealth shall conserve and maintain them for the benefit of all the people.*[173]

When this was officially signed into law, it firmly cemented Pennsylvania as a leader in environmental preservation.

Joint Resolution 3, as it was called, was popular. It was unanimously agreed on by both Republicans and Democrats; not a single congressperson opposed the bill. The new amendment was the hallmark legislation of what was labeled as the Conservation Bill of Rights in Pennsylvania. The Pennsylvania Bar Association, Pennsylvania Federation of Sportsmen's Clubs, Pennsylvania Environmental Council, League of Women Voters and the Pennsylvania Game Commission all publicly endorsed the endeavor.[174]

However, words are one matter and taking effective action is another. The power that the Twenty-Seventh Amendment would have in the legal system was still undetermined. Robert Broughton, associate professor of law at Duquesne University, described the legal implications as follows: "The amendment would effectively change the balance of legal power and give environmental quality (and the human race) at least an even chance in the coming years."[175]

Simply appending this amendment to the Pennsylvania State Constitution would not solve any environmental issue that the commonwealth was facing, and there were many. It had not yet been thirty years since Hayes led the fight against the Pittsburg, Shawmut and Northern Railroad Company. Environmental destruction from unregulated coal mining still reverberated throughout the state. Waterways were infected with industrial waste, and abandoned mines wrought unimaginable pollution on the surrounding land.

However, this addition to the constitution was an important first step to take. Del Kerr, a writer for the *Potter Enterprise*, attempted to portray the necessary solution to the conservation issue in a 1971 opinion piece:

> *Too many people think of conservation as a means of preservation. This is the wrong approach. Concession must enter the picture...for the benefit of all the people. We don't want new coal or thermal power plants because of air or water pollution. Yet we insist on more and more electrical do-dads. Automobiles reportedly cause 60 percent of all air pollution. Try carrying half-dozen bags of groceries home on a bicycle. Still, we must start somewhere to improve the environment and for our money, the Conservation Bill of Rights (Join Resolution 3) is not only a wise move, it is a necessity.*[176]

Kerr understood a principle that should have been obvious to most people: there was a tradeoff to modern innovation. The manufacturing of any product is significantly easier if there are no government standards to conform to. Therefore, many businesses operated without any significant red tape, prompting the government to gradually impose restrictions and regulations as problems arose. The U.S. government and pure capitalists learned this lesson throughout America's Gilded Age. In fact, Pennsylvania had already learned this lesson multiple times. Overhunting would have brought more species to extinction without the intervention of conservationists and the Pennsylvania Game Commission. All of Pennsylvania's vast forests would resemble deserts if it were not for the Commission of Forestry. Now Pennsylvania would have to find a way to regulate its most environmentally destructive industry yet—coal.

While deep underground mining was rarely practiced by the 1960s, strip mining started in the 1940s and is still practiced sparingly today. Strip mining is a type of surface mining in which the overlying vegetation, rock and soil is removed in order to reach the underlying coal seam, only a few feet below the surface. This practice became the new norm across Pennsylvania, as it was significantly less dangerous and imposed fewer health hazards on the miners.[177]

Strip mining was prevalent throughout this period in Bennetts Valley. However, the practice still posed a risk to the wildlife in the area. Sharing similar negative environmental effects with underground mining, strip mining destroyed natural habitats for the local wildlife and contributed to acid mine drainage, which leaked into the local watersheds.

Pennsylvania's landscape had been reshaped by human intervention for centuries, bringing many animals to the verge of extinction. In 1970, the bobcat was considered endangered, and the game commission closed the official hunting season. A predator, previously eligible for bounties, was now officially protected. The era also saw the eradication of bounties for owls and red and gray foxes.[178]

Wild turkeys received a great deal of focus from the Pennsylvania Game Commission as well. By the start of the 1960s, turkeys inhabited roughly 50 percent of the state's forest land. However, they were notably absent from the northern reaches of the state. Throughout the 1970s, birds were transported to these uninhabited areas and began to grow.

Increases in effective hunting strategies helped bolster Pennsylvania's deer and bear populations. During the late 1960s and early 1970s, extensive studies conducted by the commission's wildlife biologists showed trends in decreasing populations. These discoveries allowed the commission to properly analyze the ways in which it allocates hunting licenses and tags in specific regions. Previously, deer licenses were assigned based on "trend indices." This methodology factored in hunting results from the prior year as well as deer killed from crop damage. By 1964, the game commission had revamped its strategy. By factoring in the age of the killed deer harvested, a more accurate total for the overall herds previous year's population was calculated, which resulted in a far more precise tag allocation system. As a result, struggling deer and bear populations were protected while regions with an overabundance of the animals permitted hunting unabated.[179]

The resurgence in protecting and growing Pennsylvania's wild species became publicly noticed. Reclaiming and beautifying the lands that had been plagued by the coal mining industry was the next item on the state's agenda.

The Pennsylvania Department of Environmental Resources described the need for reclamation action in a 1976 paper that detailed the history of Pennsylvania mining practices and subsequent reclamation efforts presented at the American Society of Civil Engineers Convention.

> *As deep mining penetrated farther and farther into the earth, following the various workable veins, groundwater aquifers were intercepted. In digging for coal, other minerals are uncovered which when exposed to air and water form acids.... These acid waters invariably found their way into surface streams, either by pumping or gravity flow. The hundreds of miles of brightly colored orange stream beds and banks visible today are the result of deposits of iron and other mineral particles carried into the streams by these acid mine discharges.*[180]

Acid mine seepage occurred as long as mining was present in the state. The paper later claimed that "little control was exerted over the industry to minimize the formation of acid mine drainage." For the Valley, that meant watersheds had been polluted and inundated with acid and sulfur since the end of the nineteenth century. As Hayes would probably have said, "You can't boil out acid."

Within the same paper, the Department of Environmental Resources asserted that incredible damage was done to the surrounding ecosystem due to abandoned mines, and no effort was put forth by the companies or the state to reclaim these lands. Anywhere between 2,600 and 3,800 miles of streams were polluted by mine drainage, sewage and industrial wastes.

In 1976, there were over 100 million cubic yards of burning coal refuse banks throughout the state. Coal refuse banks are collections of low-quality coal mixed with rock, shale, slate, clay and other unused materials from previous mining operations. Due to their mineral makeup, these sites are quite susceptible to catching fire. The most famous is the Centralia refuse bank, which started burning in 1962 and is still on fire to this day. Some experts claim that the coal in the underground seam could fuel the burning for 250 more years.

At one time, the prosperous mining town in eastern Pennsylvania boasted fourteen active coal mines and over 2,500 residents. Force was a dwarf in comparison to Centralia as mining capabilities were concerned.

In May 1962, the town council was faced with an overflowing landfill. The community had a fifty-foot-deep pit covering an area about half the size of a football field. A potential solution was proposed to simply burn what

Acid mine drainage turned the color of local water sources into an orangish-brown hue.
Nicholas Tonelli, 2013.

remained in order to create room for the future. Citing its simplicity and low cost, the town council approved the idea. As a result, the fire department lined the landfill with an incombustible material, and after everything was reduced to ash, they doused the embers with water.

Everything appeared as if it had gone according to plan. Several days later, residents spotted smoke coming from the barren landfill. Upon investigation, the fire department discovered a fifteen-foot-wide hole that inadvertently connected the landfill to the labyrinth of coal mines underneath Centralia. Without physically removing everything in the landfill, there was no way to know that this entry point existed.

Lethal amounts of carbon monoxide flooded the town, and all remaining mines that were still in operation were shut down. It did not take long for the entire coal seam to catch on fire. The commonwealth tried to stop the spread of the fire multiple times. Every attempt was met with failure. Still, most residents did not leave the area until a government-led program to relocate families started in 1984.

Over twenty years had passed since the coal refuse bank caught fire, and it was believed by government officials that the residents were subjected to dangerous levels of carbon monoxide, carbon dioxide and methane. The environmental destruction was obvious: trees were dying, smoke was emitting from the ground, streets were buckling from the subsidence and the earth had transformed into ash. Before the people were forced to relocate, deer and other wild species left the area in search of a healthier habitat. The Division of Environmental Health conducted a health study on the residents of Centralia and determined that those still living in the area experienced above average levels of respiratory disease, hypertension and gastrointestinal disease. In addition, arthritis and depression were nervous system conditions that plagued the residents at an unusually high rate.[181]

Centralia was one of the most extreme cases of environmental destruction caused by the mining industry; it was a testament to the jarring extent of catastrophe made possible by the industry. In addition to the coal refuse banks, approximately 300,000 acres of deserted strip mine land were scattered throughout the state. The appearance of this acreage resembled that of an inhospitable planet; the removal of vegetation and topsoil resulted in mountains of black rock and soot with no semblance of life having ever existed there.[182]

These deplorable environmental conditions triggered the state to pass the Land and Water Conservation and Reclamation Act of 1968, which allocated $500 million in funds to the Department of Mines and Mineral

An abandoned highway near Centralia known as the "Graffiti Highway." *Wikimedia Commons, 2019.*

Resources and later the Department of Environmental Resources. Nicknamed "Operation Scarlift," referring to the desire to remove the scars of past mining practices, it was the first law in the entire country to pursue the reclamation of abandoned mining sites. The bill specifically allocated funds to improve air quality, control surface subsidence, extinguish underground fires and remove acid mine drainage from the streams. The aforementioned paper provided a record of funding allocation in the following manner:

> *The original act authorized $150 million for abatement of stream pollution, $25 million for extinguishing fires in abandoned refuse banks and $25 million for control of surface subsidence and extinguishment of underground mine fires. The Acts of July 12, 1972…approved an additional authorization of $140 million for the abatement of acid mine drainage, $20 million for the extinguishing fires in abandoned refuse banks and $40 million for the control of surface subsidence and control of underground mine fires.*[183]

Cardiff was once a principal mining operation for the PS&N. Depicted here is an abandoned strip mine in the now ghost town. *Jack Delano, 1940.*

Based on the enormous volume of capital that the state had been authorized to spend, it was clear that Pennsylvania was fully committed to restoring the natural beauty of the state.

By 1976, Operation Scarlift had achieved some successes: 48 stream miles were cleaned and a significant reduction in pollution was achieved in 140 additional miles, over 2,600 acres had been restored, 32 deep mine complexes were sealed off, 37 refuse banks had been reclaimed and 10 water treatment facilities were built and fully operational.[184] The water was cleaned by either a lime or limestone treatment process that eliminated the acid and iron pollution pertaining to the mine discharges.[185] Due to its natural purifying ability, lime was used in almost every case of water cleanup throughout the state.

While this was a step in the right direction for the environmental health of the state, much work would lie ahead. The original reclamation efforts of Operation Scarlift were conducted in or around more populated areas like Altoona, Slippery Rock, Allentown, Wilkes-Barre and Harrisburg.[186] Even though Operation Scarlift played a part in cleaning up Hawk Run near Clearfield, little to no attention other than that had been given to the rural landscape of north-central Pennsylvania where the struggling to survive elk herd lived. According to the Pennsylvania Game Commission, by 1971, the elk herd was estimated to have a population of sixty-five. The data was gathered by virtue of ground and aerial spotters, a relatively new technique in estimating wildlife populations for the time.[187]

Over the course of roughly forty years, the herd had barely grown. Unfortunately, that number soon declined to thirty-eight elk by 1974. Brain worm had spread, and it plagued the elk for a few years before finally subsiding. The parasitic infection is caused by the inadvertent consumption of snails and slugs. These gastropods live in the grassy habitats where elk feed, making the elk quite susceptible. Once ingested, the parasites start laying larvae in the bloodstream or on the outermost part of the brain. Oftentimes the newly hatched larvae are expelled from the elk via the digestive tract. However, if the larvae remain with the original parasite, they can mature into second- or third-stage larvae that can be deadly to the elk. According to the New York Department of Environmental Conservation, brain worm

> *disrupts the nervous tissue through mechanical destruction, manipulation, and inflammation. Several days after infection, the animal may have neurologic problems or abnormal behavior. After infection, there may be periods where the elk seems to recover as the worm or worms move through different portions of the brain or spinal cord. An adult parasite within the brain or spinal cord can be fatal. Death can be the result of paralysis, lack of fear/inappropriate behavior, or the inability to feed or feeding on inappropriate food items.*[188]

There have always been natural hardships that the elk faced, and this was no exception. For the elk to combat brain worm, they needed stronger immune systems, which couldn't happen with the polluted water they were forced to drink. The abhorrent environmental conditions of the Valley crippled the elk's overall health. The elk had been subjected to drinking heavily polluted water that compromised their immune systems. Clean drinking water was vital to expel the brain worm from their systems. If the elk resided in healthier areas, or perhaps if greater care was shown toward their natural habitats, then they would have been able to easily combat the parasite.[189]

Unfortunately, during this time, multiple high-ranking officials in the Pennsylvania Game Commission resigned themselves to the fact that there would never be a wide-ranging elk herd in the state and any attempts to promulgate the herd would be fruitless. If the elk herd were to survive, it would need the full support of the commission, but that would require more youthful and optimistic leaders.

Healthier habitats were already forming, and the forestry efforts spearheaded by J.T. Rothrock and Gifford Pinchot were finally seeing dividends. Throughout the state, many sections of pole timber forest were beginning to mature into saw timber. These areas provided improved forest conditions and better habitat for many wildlife species. In addition to natural forest growth, conservative and sustainable clear-cutting efforts created vast fields of shrubby vegetation and space for new saplings to grow and prosper. All of this greatly benefited grouse, deer, bears, small mammals and a multitude of birds. The investments Rothrock and Pinchot made enacting renewable forestry practices had finally paid off.

During the summer months, elk primarily live in heavily forested areas to protect themselves from the sun and heat. *Ronald J. Saffer, 2010.*

Reclamation efforts in Pennsylvania were steadily increasing but were nonetheless slow. The authors of the aforementioned paper attributed the reason behind this as the following:

> *The abatement of acid mine drainage does not lend itself to a standardized procedure. The solution to each problem must be handmade depending on the variable at the site. When one deals with inadequate and many times erroneous mine maps, fractured foundations, backfilled mine openings, underground mine pools, acid seeps, and similar conditions, it is difficult to formulate a project. Valued judgements must be made in order to determine the best and most economical solution to the problem.*[190]

Bennetts Valley would find its own handmade solution to restore abandoned mining areas. In order for the lands to be properly reclaimed, a local paper mill donated a residue byproduct that was loaded with lime. The game commission spread the material across one thousand acres of abandoned strip mine property that was a part of the state game lands in the 1980s. John Dzemyan, a game land management group supervisor who worked to restore these lands, said that "within a few years we turned

135

Throughout the Pennsylvania Wilds are many strip-mining lands reclaimed into food plots. *Wikimedia Commons, 2013.*

a barren site into a lush, green herbaceous opening."[191] In a similar way that deforested areas could provide great habitat for elk and deer, the exact same could be said about reclaimed strip mines. These clear openings would soon be filled with browse, oats and other grasses that could sustain and help nurture the elk. By 1980, the elk boasted a population of 114, tripling over a six-year period.[192] Land that was devastated by unethical mining practices was in the process of being restored, and the elk herd was reaping the benefits. However, the acid mine drainage still severely affected the local watersheds.

According to Rawland Cogan, a wildlife biologist with the Pennsylvania Game Commission at that time, in order to properly enhance elk habitat, it is important to study and understand the social nature of elk while factoring in how land manipulation affects other species. In an edition of *Pennsylvania Game News*, Cogan described the studies he and his team performed:

> *Since 1982, to better understand when and why elk use various types of habitat, we've used radio-telemetry to monitor movements of 170 different elk. We've learned that habitat use varies based on topography, vegetation type, aspect and slope, along with time of day and season of the year. These*

Reclaimed strip mine lands in Cardiff are now home to a growing American chestnut tree population. *Wikimedia Commons, 2014.*

factors are compounded by sex, age, herding instinct and learned (past) experiences. More specifically we've learned that elk use larger (8 to 20 acre) openings more often than smaller (less than 8 acres) ones, and that if we developed several openings totaling 40 to 60 acres within a 5 squared mile area (referred to as complexes) that elk would live there most of the year traveling from one of those openings to another, in this complex. This is one of the ways we've reduced elk movements to agricultural areas.[193]

Due to the rising elk population, the newly reclaimed lands were pursued by the Pennsylvania Game Commission for elk habitat purposes. As the herd grew in size, so did complaints about elk destroying and eating crops. In 1982, the commission announced that it would hold a lottery for a new elk hunting season to rectify some of the issues the growing herd was causing. This would be the first time elk could be legally hunted in Pennsylvania since 1931. The goal of the proposed hunt was to cut the herds' size by awarding thirty tags to lucky sportsmen. However, during 1982, fifteen elk were shot illegally, eleven were killed for crop damage and nine others died of various causes. This hit to the elk population eliminated the need for an elk hunt, and the plans were abandoned as a result.[194]

In the wake of the failed 1982 hunting season, crop damage complaints did not subsist. The creation of state game lands would be one solution to help quell this persisting problem. These new areas would lure elk away from private farms and into public lands. Farmers and landowners were instructed by the Pennsylvania Game Commission on how to make their lands less susceptible to crop damage; the new methods ranged from constructing fences to planting crop mixtures that elk were less likely to eat.

Cogan was personally involved in implementing measures to mitigate negative elk to human interactions. Near farms surrounding eastern St. Marys, high-tensile steel fencing was constructed to prevent crop damage by elk, deer and bears. Additionally, Cogan conducted crop depredation surveys to gauge losses to wildlife. In these studies, Cogan visited each affected landowner and estimated monetary damages based on the acreage and the average yield price for corn, oats, winter wheat, hay mix, alfalfa or whatever crop was destroyed.[195]

Additionally, the Pennsylvania Game Commission started to engage in education programs throughout the state as a necessity for the future of conservation. By the late 1980s, the game commission was spending about $100,000 each year to develop educational materials to distribute to schools and residents across the commonwealth. Lantz Hoffman, the director of the agency's Bureau of Information, praised the new direction that the commission was undertaking:

> *The children who will benefit from this service are Pennsylvania's tomorrow and represent our future natural resource caretakers. It's important they know what's out there and understand how priceless wildlife and other natural resources are.*[196]

The new focus on educational programs allowed the Pennsylvania Game Commission to become the foremost authority on wildlife education in the state. For years, many residents made ignorant cries to the state government and the commission, claiming that the wild game populations were growing out of control. Most specifically, attention was drawn to Pennsylvania's deer population. In the late 1980s, Steve Liscinsky, a wildlife biologist for the commission, described his interpretation of residents' complaints about contemporary game management strategies:

> *In recent years, Game Commission employees, especially research biologists, have been battered with increasing cries of "too many deer." As one would suspect, these cries are not coming from hunters but rather from farmers,*

*foresters, and motorists. This is not a new complaint as such, since there
have been outcries of this nature since the 1920s. But what is new are the
current outcries in light of an ever-improving management program. Those
who make the most noise seem to have the least knowledge or appreciation
of the hard struggle which was required to get a good deer control program
underway. Perhaps they haven't been around as long as some of us, or
perhaps no one ever told them how bad it was.*[197]

The commission's investment into education programs would help solve
the annoyance perceived by Liscinsky. They believed that if the population is
well educated on the subject of wildlife conservation and its history, then there
would be less ignorant cries from the public. The game commission would
teach the history of the commonwealth's conservation efforts, which enabled
residents of the state to gain a greater appreciation for their natural wildlife.

By the 1990s, it was believed that the elk population had eclipsed the
two hundred mark. Wildlife education conducted by the Pennsylvania
Game Commission taught state residents the history of conservation as well
as the practices employed by the commission. The newly educated public
and revitalized land provided the foundation that allowed the elk herd to
continually grow throughout the last decade of the twentieth century.

An increased usage of biological studies in the preceding decade was a
major contributing factor for the steady growth in population. Cogan was
directly involved in calf survival, mortality and disease studies conducted by
the game commission. In a 1998 edition of *Pennsylvania Game News*, Cogan
described the importance of calf survival studies:

*Knowing how many calves cow elk are likely to produce is important for
predicting population trends, which, in turn enables us to plan habitat
enhancement, trap and transfer and other herd control projects. In 1991 we
started instrumenting adult cows (2 or more years old) with radio transmitters
and then monitoring them during the calving seasons. We tracked cows by
vehicle, on horseback and on foot, to determine if a calf had been born. We
knew the age and capture location of each cow we tracked.*

Cogan went on to share the results of the studies conducted throughout
the decade:

*During our study we monitored 161 adult cows. Reproductive rates for
1991–1997 ranged from 54 percent to 88 percent and averaged 68*

percent. Based on this data, the most productive cows were those 3 to 10 years of age. The oldest cow to produce a calf was 16. She produced a calf 5 of 7 years of the study. Of the 144 births and pregnancies documented, 141 were single calves. We observed twins only three times. In two instance, the twins were alive, apparently healthy. In the third, in 1994, a cow gave birth to stillborn twins. That cow died about two weeks later, most likely due to injuries occurred during birthing and from infection.

The breadth of knowledge that Cogan and the Pennsylvania Game Commission acquired was vital to conserving the future of the state's elk herd. This data was never before available, and it allowed conservationists to make the best possible decisions for the future of the state's wildlife. Now armed with new knowledge, Cogan believed that elk did have a future within the state and started to convince others within the Pennsylvania Game Commission.[198]

Private institutions also assisted the commission in its efforts to protect Pennsylvania's elk herd. One of the biggest examples of cooperation surfaced during this time. The Rocky Mountain Elk Foundation (RMEF) contributed $38,000 to the 1990 purchase of State Game Lands 311, which was a 1,600-acre tract of land on top of Winslow Hill near Benezette. The area was eventually reclaimed and rebranded as an elk viewing area, where travelers from across the country could come see the elk in their natural habitat. Today, State Game Lands 311 covers nearly 3,800 acres and is incorporated into the primary range of Pennsylvania's elk herd.[199]

The RMEF is a national organization dedicated to the conservation of elk throughout North America. It has helped restore elk populations in West Virginia, Virginia, Missouri, North Carolina, Tennessee, Kentucky, Wisconsin and even Ontario, Canada. RMEF accomplishes its conservation goals by acquiring and transforming land into quality protected habitats that produce nutritious food for elk and other wildlife.

In the early 1990s, it was RMEF's turn to help Pennsylvania's elk herd thrive. After its initial investment, the RMEF donated an additional $92,000 toward elk management. The money, which was gathered through the foundation's fundraising efforts, was allocated to habitat enhancement and the construction of electric fences that would deter elk from wandering onto agricultural lands. The partnership between RMEF and the Pennsylvania Game Commission would greatly improve the quality of life of the elk for many years to come.[200]

Many other private organizations helped the commission by purchasing and reclaiming habitat throughout the 1980s and 1990s. During this

Areas on Winslow Hill, one of the premiere destinations for elk tourists, are reclaimed strip-mining sites. *Bob Traveny, 1990s.*

time, the Pennsylvania Game Commission pursued an aggressive land acquisition program in order to protect as many wild areas as possible. However, the commission was limited due to the rising cost of land and, as a result, relied on private conservation organizations that could afford the expensive land purchases. For reference, the average price per acre had risen from $10 in the 1920s to $400 in 1994. Inflation during this span made $10 in 1920 as valuable as $75 in 1994; the price of land more than quadrupled past the rate of inflation. Though prices did vary based on the property's location within the state.

Thankfully, areas in north-central Pennsylvania were relatively cheap compared to lands near the Pocono Mountains, which were considered to be a part of the greater New York metropolitan area. The commission was able to purchase some land but was unable to acquire all that was necessary to achieve its conservation goals. Some of the generous organizations include the Western Pennsylvania Conservancy, Wildlands Conservancy, Seneca Highlands Conservancy, Nature Conservancy, French and Pickering Creek Land Conservation Trust, Northern Allegheny Conservation Association, Trust for Public Lands, National Fish and Wildlife Foundation, Ducks Unlimited, Waterfowl USA, National Wild Turkey Federation and the Rocky Mountain Elk Foundation.[201]

Nature tourists throughout the state had begun to take notice of Pennsylvania's elk herd. The population was rising, and people wanted to see what was widely considered to be an animal that lived only in the western reaches of the United States. In 1995, the *Daily News*, out of Huntingdon, published an article that described the current state of elk tourism. The author, Wes Bower, recounted his perception of elk watching in the Valley:

> *Sportsmen wishing to see and hear the rutting elk in September and October should head north of Benezette in Elk County. The herds are usually observed feeding on new grass in the large reclaimed strip mines. Ask questions of local residents and business establishments. Look for a number of cars parked in the same area. Sometimes the elk can be observed from your vehicle. Other times, a short hike is necessary. Citizen band radios are the "in" thing with elk viewers and the word is quickly transmitted when elk are spotted....Pennsylvania's elk are a unique resource. It's probable that this commonwealth's elk population will never attain the numbers which would make hunting these critters a viable program. That's OK. There's more to the sport of hunting than killing a trophy critter. Having these oversized deer within the state's borders reminds us that truly wild things still roam our fields and forests. Listening to, and seeing, these noble animals continues to be an exciting outdoor adventure.[202]*

Elk were becoming a spectacle that many outdoor enthusiasts from across the state wanted to witness firsthand. The *Indiana Gazette* claimed that in 2001 over seventy thousand people visited the viewing areas in Benezette Township. The article also indicated that residents of the Valley were irate about the increased tourism because many visitors "who—seeing an elk in someone's back yard or on the side of the road—simply stop, rush out of their cars with their cameras, tie up traffic and trespass on private land."[203] This posed not only a privacy problem for residents but also a safety hazard for others driving through the Valley. Seemingly overnight, thousands of tourists were flooding the rural community.

Overcrowding became such an issue that the Department of Conservation and Natural Resources (DCNR) formed an agency coined the "Elk Patrol." Terry Brady, a spokesman for DCNR, said that the idea behind the Elk Patrol

> *is not to add more law enforcement or to ticket people; instead, it is to use the Game Commission Officers and forest rangers already in the area in concert*

with state police to keep traffic moving and people off private property. In the village of Benezette itself, they're under the gun when the viewing season begins in earnest.[204]

This was a good problem to have, because it meant that the elk herd along with the rest of the area's wildlife was thriving and people from across the state were beginning to take note of it.

In order to safely accommodate the new influx of tourism to the incredibly rural region, multiple state game lands were branded as elk viewing areas. Onlookers could observe the elk grazing in open fields from areas that were accessible by car. The Winslow Hill Elk Viewing Area and Dents Run Elk Viewing Area near Benezette and the Hoover Farm Viewing Area and Hicks Run Viewing Area near Driftwood are some of the more popular elk observing spots in the region.

In 2001, thanks to the removal of the mines, beautification of the land and a public education push, the herd was estimated to be about seven hundred strong. The rapid expansion of the herd's size may be largely credited to a trap and transfer program initiated by the Pennsylvania Game Commission. In order to transport the massive animals, calves, cows and small spike bulls were corralled, while large bulls were anesthetized.

Cars flood the streets of Benezette on a September night during the rut. *Willard Hill, 2020.*

Visitors crowd the already narrow streets near Benezette to view a lone cow. *Willard Hill, 2016.*

Prior to the trap and transfer initiative in 1997, the elk herd occupied a tract of land of approximately two hundred square miles in southeastern Elk and western Cameron Counties. The goal of the program was to redistribute sixty to ninety elk to new regions in Clearfield and Clinton Counties and to increase the occupied area to eight hundred square miles. Calvin DuBrock, director of the Pennsylvania Game Commission at the time, described the program as a necessity for the future of the Pennsylvania elk because they were naturally migrating to more urban areas—where they would get killed. The commission wanted to redirect the elk to state lands in order to limit human interactions.

> *If they head north or southwest we're certain to have conflicts. We'd prefer they'd just head south and east where there's a large public land base, lower human densities, virtually no farming and no state highways.*[205]

Upon engaging in trap and transfer, the Pennsylvania Game Commission killed two birds with one stone. It was able to facilitate the rapid growth of the elk herd while also limiting the amount of negative human interactions.

With some of these newly transferred elk being fitted with radio collars, it was easy to determine if any of the animals attempted to head back to their original territory. While no elk permanently returned to their original tract, interesting data was collected that described how far they eventually wandered. According to Cogan,

> *By the end of the study, the farthest movement of any translocated elk we know was the 38.9 air miles where one bull traveled to Germania. Another unusual movement was by an adult cow that moved 22 air miles south of the holding pen. The cow later returned to the Sinnemahoning valley within a few miles of the holding pen. Another adult cow moved 18 miles west to an area within a mile of her capture site. She spent several days with other elk using the area and then went back to within four miles of the release site and gave birth to a calf. After a month or so of their release, most elk had settled into their new surroundings.*[206]

Disease studies were also beginning to show encouraging results for the herd. According to Cogan, the game commission tested for brucellosis, tuberculosis, chronic wasting disease and the infamous brain worm. A special brain worm study that was conducted from 1982 to 2002 showed that less than 1 percent of elk mortalities could be contributed to the parasite—a significant relief considering it nearly decimated the herd in the early 1970s.

It was at this point that nearly every biological factor that affected the elk no longer posed a major threat to their survival. Through these revelations among the many studies conducted by Cogan and the Pennsylvania Game Commission, it was revealed that one of the last great barriers was not a natural deterrent but a sociological one. In other words, if the elk herd was to expand past its current mark, Pennsylvanians needed to become comfortable with them living in their vicinity.

Fully aware of this, in 1997, the Pennsylvania Game Commission officially stated that its elk management goal was

> *to recognize elk as a valuable wildlife resource, and to perpetuate a free-roaming elk population within suitable habitat for viewing and unique hunting opportunities at levels compatible with habitat capacities that affected landowners will accept.*[207]

The game commission made it clear that the preservation of the elk herd was a major priority. By this time, the herd was estimated to be about three hundred strong, and in 2001, the herd more than doubled in size via the trap and transfer program. However, the elk viewing areas and lands used for the trap and transfer relocation, while beautiful and proudly reclaimed, was still surrounded by severely polluted waterways from acid mine drainage.

Elk were now thriving on newly protected state lands, and many people had begun to take note. However, that did not mean that the scars inflicted from the mining industry were completely healed. Pennsylvania's waterways still suffered from severe acid mine drainage. The streams in the elk's primary range throughout north-central Pennsylvania suffered the most.

The largest body of water in the region, and subsequently the most affected area of acid mine drainage, was the Bennetts Branch of the Sinnemahoning. Covering thirty-eight miles in total length, the lower thirty-three miles were severely affected by mining pollution. An incredible amount of water flows through this watershed; according to the Pennsylvania Department of Environmental Protection, the average daily flow at the mouth of the stream near Driftwood is 454 million gallons per day. Nearly 70 percent of the area surrounding the watershed is either State Forest Lands or State Game Lands.

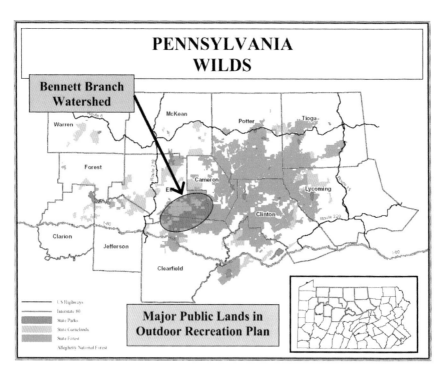

Overview of recreational public lands in the Pennsylvania Wilds. *Pennsylvania Department of Environmental Protection, 2010.*

It was not until 2004 that the pollution of the Bennetts Branch Watershed was finally addressed. While Operation Scarlift was officially over by the mid-1970s, it took nearly thirty years for the state to start cleaning up the acid mine drainage in the area. Nevertheless, help had finally arrived. In the first year, approximately 150 sampling stations were erected at multiple locations along the watershed to identify the regions most contributing to the stream's contamination.[208] It was determined that the areas near Hollywood and Tyler, two mining villages no farther than two miles south of Force, contributed the most acid to the Bennetts Branch—about 41 percent of the total load. Two other main locations were also identified: the Caledonia Run Subbasin, contributing 24 percent, and the Dents Run Subbasin, contributing 27 percent of the acid load. In total, the state determined that there would need to be thirty-six projects located in twenty-five severely problematic areas.[209]

Eric Cavazza, the acting chief of the Division of Acid Mine Drainage for the Pennsylvania Department of Environmental Protection, claimed that

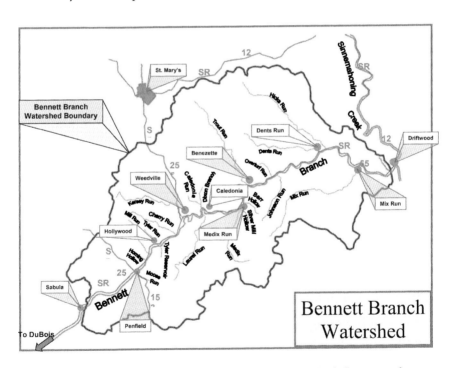

Map of tributaries within the Bennett's Branch watershed. *Pennsylvania Department of Environmental Protection, 2010.*

by 2010 much progress had been made to restore the Bennetts Branch watershed. In January of that year, twenty of the thirty-six initially proposed projects were completed at a cost in excess of $19 million; five more projects were under construction that would cost just below $5 million; four projects were currently under design and would cost nearly $18 million; and the seven projects that were still left to be planned were estimated at $4.5 million.[210]

The Hollywood Treatment Plant was the most expensive venture pursued by the Department of Environmental Protection. The $14.6 million plant used hydrated lime and sludge recirculation technology to treat the surrounding water. The facility was and is still cleaning 8.6 million gallons of water per day. By 2012, the main streams of the Bennetts Branch Watershed were free of all acid mine drainage.

For the first time in over one hundred years, the water was finally capable of sustaining aquatic life. Jeff Mulhoelm of *Outdoor News* gleefully exclaimed, "A trout river had been reborn."[211] Although native species of trout, eel and aquatic insects, among others, would never naturally return, the stream revitalization was a sign that Pennsylvania was on the right path to reclaiming itself. Since 2012, trout stocking organizations have committed many resources to restoring the local populations, and in 2021, the Bennetts Valley Sportsmen's Club, under the leadership of Troy Huff, was created with the sole initiative to keep the streams of Bennetts Valley stocked with trout for local fishermen.

The streams that President Grant had vacationed to on three separate occasions were on their way to being fully reclaimed. Not only was it possible that life could sustain itself in these streams, but the Valley finally had a clean source of water for its local wildlife as well. Perhaps, with the streams finally providing clean water, the elk would be able to prosper at their full potential.

The elk herd's population grew throughout the 2000s. In 2001, the Pennsylvania Game Commission reinstated annual elk hunts, which continue to this day. The elk hunts served a few purposes. First, the continually recurring issue of farmers complaining to the state about crop damage was formally addressed. Second, since the herd was significantly more durable and able to withstand a hunting season, harvesting a certain number of elk would benefit the species in the long run. Older animals do not breed as often as their more youthful counterparts yet consume food and other resources that the younger elk vitally need. The hunts allowed the herd to repopulate at a much higher rate.[212] In the first year of hunts, 27 elk were harvested,

Aerial view of the completed Hollywood AMD Treatment Plant. *Pennsylvania Department of Environmental Protection, 2013.*

and after the conclusion of the 2012 season, 509 elk, cumulatively, had been legally hunted.[213] With the waterways finally clean after over one hundred years of pollution and a thriving ecotourism industry, the future was looking bright for Pennsylvania's elk.

Operation Scarlift and Pennsylvania's Twenty-Seventh Amendment signaled to many a change in course for the path of the commonwealth's conservation and environment policies. Although it took nearly forty years for these efforts to reach the heart of Elk Country, help had finally arrived for one of the state's most historic natural resources. That help manifested itself as a partnership of private and government organizations, which in tandem were able to protect the wildlife of Pennsylvania in a manner that they could only accomplish through continued cooperation.

6

A NEW SONG FOR AN OLD FOREST

*I*n 2007, Pennsylvania governor Ed Rendell convened a two-day "Outdoor Conference" in State College. Revolutionary technological innovations like smartphones and the internet had cemented themselves into everyday life, and Rendell was concerned about mitigating the potential negative effects. The goal of this conference was to devise a strategy to help Pennsylvanians reconnect with nature. Rendell believed that Americans of all ages were becoming increasingly more insulated from the great Pennsylvania Wilds and that this sociological divide could threaten the physical health, emotional well-being and environmental quality of Pennsylvania's communities.[214]

The biggest outcome from this conference was, without a doubt, an initiative to create the Elk Country Visitor Center in Benezette. Governor Rendell believed that the

> *center will bring a double benefit to north-central Pennsylvania. It will boost nature tourism in the region, but it will also deliver a conservation message that it is up to us to preserve our wild and natural areas.*[215]

The Rocky Mountain Elk Foundation purchased land at the top of Winslow Hill, which was owned by Jim and Barb Betta, who operated a Christmas Tree farm on the premises. Winslow Hill was also the site of the first settlers to come to Elk County. Governor Rendell wanted the viewing center to be a world-class destination for people from across the globe to visit

The Elk Country Visitors Center welcomes nearly half a million visitors annually. *Wikimedia Commons, 2014.*

and experience the great Pennsylvania outdoors. As a result, he pledged $5 million in state funds for construction in coordination with RMEF's efforts.[216]

The Elk Country Visitor Center is not just a building but an eco-friendly educational complex. The 8,400-square-foot facility houses many interactive displays that teach visitors all about elk and other aspects of Pennsylvania wildlife. Some of these attractions include a scale that visitors can step on and compare their weight with that of an elk, while video monitors and interactive displays instruct how to identify grasses that the elk enjoy eating. The biggest attraction inside the center is the 4D movie theater, where visitors can spend roughly thirty minutes and learn a brief history of Pennsylvania's elk herd. Surrounding the center are multiple walking trails that traverse the Winslow Hill property.

According to the Elk Country Visitor Center's website, the overall design of the complex was made with energy efficiency, environmental conservation and minimizing ecological impacts in mind.

The location and layout of the building and parking lot were chosen to minimize the facility's impact on the ecosystem. The building itself features energy efficient materials and designs, solar-oriented windows for warmth and lighting, and a renewable geothermal heating and cooling system. Materials used to construct the facility contained recycled content, and remaining materials were sorted, recycled, and donated to the local community for firewood, crafts and other uses. The Center collects and recycles rainwater for use in the building's restroom facilities. And of course, we ask all visitors to properly dispose of recyclables and trash while on the property.[217]

The Elk Country Visitor Center was not the only destination that the state heavily invested in during this time. In 2011, the Sinnemahoning State Park Visitor Center and the Kinzua Bridge Visitor Center officially opened their doors to the public. The location in Sinnemahoning is home to over 1,900 acres of beautiful scenery and wildlife habitat. Focusing on the vast biodiversity of wildlife within Pennsylvania's forests, the visitor center in Sinnemahoning's main goal is to further educate the public on conservation efforts throughout the state.[218] However, the Kinzua Bridge State Park's motive is to retell the construction, history and legacy of the Kinzua Bridge, which was destroyed in 2003 by a tornado that swept through the region. At one time, the railroad on the bridge was the longest and tallest to span a valley in the state.[219] Like the Elk Country Visitor Center, both of these facilities were built with energy efficiency and environmental conservation in mind. More importantly, these facilities underscored the incredible efforts that the State of Pennsylvania willingly engaged in to help spread the need for conservation efforts across the world.

While the announcement for the Elk Country Visitor Center came in 2007, it did not open until September 2010. In the meantime, the Great Recession severely affected many working-class Americans throughout the country. The Valley and the heart of Elk Country was no exception. Luckily for them, their biggest export, elk tourism, was steadily increasing and as a result would inject much-needed capital into the area. Perhaps due to Governor Rendell's announcement, the existing elk viewing areas were becoming overcrowded. Regardless of the visitor center being built, Benezette was drawing large amounts of tourism dollars. According to the Pennsylvania Great Outdoors Visitor Bureau, elk watching and nature tourism provided $250 million to the Pennsylvania Wilds region to date.[220] By spending money directly at the visitor center, dining in local establishments, patronizing nearby businesses and lodging in surrounding hotels, tourists brought new wealth during a difficult time.

Unfortunately, due to the 2008 housing market crash, Rendell lost a partner. Strapped financially, the RMEF backed out of its efforts in north-central Pennsylvania. In order to fill the void left, Rawland Cogan, a wildlife biologist who had worked for the Pennsylvania Game Commission and the Rocky Mountain Elk Foundation, formed the Keystone Elk Country Alliance (KECA) to take over all of RMEF's responsibilities.

Since then, the Elk Country Visitor Center has been maintained by KECA, a 501(c)(3) nonprofit wildlife conservation organization that focuses its efforts on preserving and protecting Pennsylvania's elk herd.[221] In accordance with Governor Rendell's desire for the visitor center to be a leading authority on conservation education, KECA actively strives to educate as many visitors as possible. It provides on-site learning opportunities through its outdoor classroom facilities; distance learning seminars for schools; and many different educational programs for people of all ages. In fact, the popularity surrounding on-site learning has grown significantly since the center opened. An outdoor classroom was constructed near the center that allows employees and volunteers to teach in a more accommodating area.

The viability of Pennsylvania's elk herd would not be what it is today without the continuing support of KECA. Over the past decade, it has made great strides in advancing wildlife conservation and education. Rawland Cogan, the president and CEO of KECA, described the alliance's conservation efforts as a three-pronged approach: conservation education, land enhancement and permanent land protection. Cogan described conservation education as

> *our number one priority. We have this world class destination, the Elk Country Visitor Center. We are attracting between 400,000 and 500,000 people a year....So when you have a destination like that we use it to our advantage to educate people about Elk Country. That's why they are coming here. They want to see more but they also want to be educated. They want to learn about this animal, where they live, what they eat, how they breed, how they survive, and how man lives with them.*[222]

KECA has professional educators that do programming year-round and are connected with school districts nationwide. Elk education is the foundation on which the Elk Country Visitor Center was built so that a greater respect and appreciation for elk and their habitat can be fostered and maintained.

Land enhancement is also an important aspect of KECA's mission. According to Cogan, his organization enhances around 400 acres of land per year and so far has managed to enhance 4,500 unique acres in total. Land enhancement can mean anything from mowing to planting high-quality forage to negotiating special deals with private landowners and farmers.

Cogan asserted that mowing is actually "one of the most effective treatments we can do. It keeps the weeds down and creates lush green vegetation. It's more nutritious for the elk."[223]

In one specific instance, KECA negotiated with a landowner near Kettle Creek who makes and sells hay to horse owners. This area was, and still is, vital for future elk generations because it is situated in a rural habitat that elk can take advantage of without having to worry about human contact. Cogan explained,

> Rather than us going there and planting a clover plot, which horses eat but it's not preferred; we went in and planted in a hay mix for horses. And the landowner agrees not to make hay on it until July 1, which gives the fawns a chance to grow and get mobile.…He takes one cutting off of those fields a year and the rest of it is there for the wildlife.[224]

Private land management is a niche that KECA actively pursues. Oftentimes there are landowners who are land rich and cash poor, and they do not necessarily have the tools or expertise to create good, lush habitats for wildlife.

KECA's third prong, permanent land protection, is simply the practice of purchasing land and cultivating it as fertile ground for wildlife. Permanent land protection is a relatively expensive endeavor, which KECA cannot often afford to pursue. However, Cogan stated that it is important because

> a lot of conservation groups will go out and protect an acre…and they'll flip it to the state. That's all well and good as long as the state can take care of it, and right now they've got so much. They can't get to all of it. It just makes more sense for a group like the Keystone Elk Country Alliance to maintain their own sort of sect.[225]

Because KECA is not government-controlled, it can achieve goals specific to elk management that the state is not able to devote enough attention to. Governor Rendell's initial plans and hopes for the Elk Country Visitor's Center would not have been achieved without the conservation efforts pursued by KECA and other similar organizations like RMEF. Additionally, elk tourism and the wealth accompanying it would not have found their way into the Pennsylvania Wilds.

Over the first decade of the twenty-first century, Benezette, a town of less than 200 people, consistently averaged a yearly tourism rate of nearly

Battle at Ruffo Flats by American artist David Anderson.

70,000 people. Governor Rendell hoped that, by 2016, the new visitor center would significantly increase this number to 160,000 visitors annually.[226] Throughout the four months following the opening, the center welcomed approximately 55,000 tourists. During the center's first full year of operation in 2011, around 217,000 people came to learn more about Pennsylvania's great elk herd. In 2019 alone, the visitor center welcomed over 520,000 tourists to Benezette.[227] As of today, the Elk Country Visitor Center has welcomed visitors from all fifty states and forty-five countries from around the world. The public's swift engagement and interest in the center was a true testament to the value of wildlife conservation and education. The foresight of the State of Pennsylvania and Governor Rendell in recognizing the popularity of wildlife tourism would prove to be incredibly beneficial to the state and Bennetts Valley as a whole.

The economic benefits that elk tourism brought the region are made readily apparent to the local residents. From Benezette to Weedville, multiple new stores that focus on promoting elk tourism opened their doors within the past few years. One of the most prominent new businesses, Elk Life, is located in the heart of downtown Benezette and sells elk-themed apparel. Additionally, the influx of tourism dollars has rejuvenated existing businesses in the area like the Benezette Hotel & Restaurant, which has become a staple of the community.

Local residents have experienced improvements in their everyday lives that can be directly attributed to the ecotourism industry. Over the past few years, cell towers have been built throughout the Valley, giving the community access to mobile phone service providers. The first was built in

Driftwood, and another tower was inaugurated in Weedville in the spring of 2022. Additionally, property value has seen a significant rise over the past few decades. As the popularity of the region increased, so, too, has the demand for real estate grown.

While everything was boding well for the region from a financial aspect, that did not mean the elk herd was now invincible. Most recently, a wave of chronic wasting disease (CWD) began to spread in nearby areas, mainly among the deer population. A degenerative neurological disorder, CWD is always fatal and is known to spread among deer, elk, reindeer and moose populations. Although CWD has not yet affected any major portion of Pennsylvania's elk population, it is only a matter of time before cases begin.

Cogan painted the picture of CWD threatening the elk herd in the following manner:

> CWD is on our doorstep....There are many that believe that it's not a matter of if, but a matter of when. There have been cases just south near I-80, and we just had a CWD positive deer out in western elk county. It is on our southern and western borders.[228]

It is possible that members of the elk herd could travel to these areas, where they would be in contact with infected deer.

Philip Tome once described elk as the nomads of the forest, and that is especially true when bull elk create bastard groups. These small packs of male elk form because they were not strong enough to win control over a harem of cows from another bull. Cogan claimed that for the past three or four years, bastard elk that traveled into known CWD areas have been shot by the game commission. The fear is that on returning to the main range in the heart of Elk Country, these animals could spread CWD to the rest of the herd. "Currently that is our biggest threat to the survival of Elk Country," claimed Cogan.[229]

However, Cogan represents a slightly more optimistic view. While recognizing the looming threat of CWD, he believes that the elk herd is strong enough to survive.

> CWD has been all around us for years. If you don't look for it you don't know it is there. If you start testing, then it pops up. I'm not convinced it hasn't been around before.[230]

Cogan's optimism stems from his personal and professional experiences. He has hunted all across the United States in CWD regions. He claimed that while hunting regulations are different in these areas, the deer and elk populations still survive.

KECA and the Pennsylvania Game Commission actively learn from CWD-affected areas and study which methods are most effective at mitigating the spread of the virus. Some of these remedies should not come as too much of a surprise—for example, quarantining.

While CWD poses a grave threat to the elk herd, they will more than likely survive. It is incredibly likely that the herd has already survived it in the past. In Cogan's words, "It could be the death of Elk Country, but it can't be. We wouldn't let it happen."[231] The revenue that has already been generated for the State of Pennsylvania and for conservation projects at large is reason enough to use every resource available to save the herd.

Cogan adamantly believes that even if CWD affects the elk herd, the population will continue to grow. He estimates that the herd could climb to north of 1,500 by 2024. The current range for the elk herd can support 3,000 to 3,500 elk. The only factor preventing it from growing further is the people. "It then becomes a matter of how willing people are to live with the elk," claimed Cogan.[232] For the people in the Valley, it would not be much to ask at all. However, other regions that have not fostered elk populations in two centuries may not be as willing. It is human nature to repel change, especially changes to everyday life and customs. That will be the challenge that needs to be addressed when the time comes, and it may not be too long from now.

Eco-tourism clearly provided a great deal of wealth and recognition for Bennetts Valley, as well as giving Pennsylvanians an opportunity to have a career in their own backyards. "It is much better than the alternative. What would you rather do, go to work in a carbon plant or one of Pennsylvania's wildlife destinations?" asked Cogan rhetorically.[233] The spectacle of the region as a reclaimed wonder of Pennsylvania's history in tandem with the natural awe of the elk herd brought hundreds of millions of wealth to the area, and it is only getting better.

However, I fear that as the elk continue to grow in popularity they will come to be viewed as nothing more than a simple attraction—not entirely unlike how Philip Tome captured live elk and toured them across the countryside and allowed only those who paid a fee to view the animals. Nonetheless, I remain hopeful that Pennsylvania will not succumb to folly and allow profit streams to dictate its ongoing conservation pursuits. If the state does not, it will have fallen victim to the same misguided ideologies that allowed overhunting to exterminate many species, unsustainable logging to clear-cut every great forest and reprehensible coal mining practices to severely pollute the natural environment.

—⁓—

IN THE SUMMER OF 2021, my family and I went on a vacation to Bar Harbor, Maine, which is situated right outside of Acadia National Park. Bar Harbor, while small in geographic terms, is home to a bustling and flourishing eco-tourism economy because of its natural wildlife and many hiking trails. Known for its lobster industry and its beautifully maintained national parks, it is easy to forget that Bar Harbor was once a simple town with no attractions at all. When Acadia National Park was established, slowly but surely the tourism economy found its way to Bar Harbor. When I went there, I became ensconced in the scenery, and promptly acted like a tourist, buying T-shirts and going on guided wildlife tours.

At one point, I turned to my sister and said, "Wouldn't it be great if the elk became just as popular as Bar Harbor?" In utter disagreement, she replied, "No, I don't want Benezette and Weedville to turn into a big tourist trap filled with hotels and people selling homemade T-shirts on the street." When she said that, I realized she was right. If the Valley became the next Bar Harbor, it would lose focus on the years of conservation efforts that so many people throughout the state fought for. Pennsylvania needs to stay focused on conservation and not the pursuit of wealth. That does not mean money cannot be earned along the way; it just cannot be the main guiding principle.

When I interviewed Cogan for this book, I asked him if he worried about the Valley becoming a second-rate tourist attraction.

Our whole idea from the beginning, and I'm going back twelve, fifteen years before [the Elk Country Visitor Center] *was even built, we had meetings and open houses and just had a lot of discussion about this and what I said was "Benezette is this quaint little town sitting out in the middle of the woods. It had everything from timber to a coal mining town; hunting and fishing and all the outdoors. It needs to maintain its sense of place. It is the attraction because of what it is, where it is and how it operates. If it becomes the same as every other tourist town, then it loses its sense of place." So what I suggested is that Benezette figures out a way to maintain its sense of place, but still taking advantage of the tourism dollars from people coming here.*[234]

It is important for KECA and the residents of the Valley that their area maintains its core identity—a rural community that lives side by side with nature. Tourists from urban areas travel to Elk Country not only to see the elk but also to experience the rural community lifestyle. They see the vast ruralness of the Pennsylvania Wilds as a peaceful yet exotic endeavor to reconnect with nature. An odyssey composed of magnificently beautiful natural landscapes, clean air and water and some of the clearest night skies in the entire world.

There is a reason people moved to Benezette and still live there today. It is a town of only 180 people. Over the past few years, there has been some turnover of residents moving out, and others have come in to take advantage of the elk tourism industry. Cogan eventually reiterated his desire by saying,

> *What we want to see is Benezette remain this quaint little town in the middle of the woods now…and I'm just going to say it straight up, Benezette has been able to do that, because there is no infrastructure here.…There's no way a hotel chain can come in here because they can't get enough water.*[235]

If Benezette and the rest of the Valley do not stay true to their identity, then nearly every effort to revive the area will have been made in vain. Luckily for the region, a massive barrier blocks any chance of major development: no access to large quantities of water. Cogan went on to say that during the best months out of the year, the Elk Country Visitor Center can pump only eight gallons of water per day. Barring a massive infrastructure investment, no major retail or hotel chains could ever consider construction in Benezette.

What the area has instead seen are hotels being built in bigger towns within twenty to forty minutes of Benezette—DuBois, St. Marys, Clearfield and Emporium, to name a few. These towns have also benefited from the elk tourism industry without endangering their own identities. Unlike the Valley, another hotel in any of those towns won't affect their way of life. Therefore, Benezette has been able to maintain its sense of place while also spreading the influx of wealth to the surrounding areas that can easily handle, and are not bothered by, the extra people.

The surge of tourists and money to the region has resulted in many communities adopting the iconography of the elk for advertisement and business purposes. A brochure for the St. Marys Chamber of Commerce reads, "St. Marys, Come Visit Pennsylvania's Elk Herd." The text lays atop a picture of a mature bull elk. The problem therein is that the elk do not live in St. Marys; in fact, they never have. Since their reintroduction, only a few nomadic elk have ever ventured into that area, and when a sizable herd did get close to the town, the residents and farmers started to shoot and kill the elk. After tensions reached an all-time high, the Pennsylvania Game Commission relocated the elk toward the Lock Haven area. The elk herd has never been a part of the culture of St. Marys, yet an official city marketing document was proclaiming to the world the elk were a primary reason to visit. St. Marys understood that it could capitalize on the tourism dollars that are coming into the Weedville and Benezette areas and through careful marketing can recruit tourists to their city.

The elk herd is the identity of Benezette and Bennetts Valley at large. It took over two hundred years' worth of mistakes for the people of the Valley to realize how important their local environment and the elk herd are and how that journey cements their place in history. When species were overhunted throughout Pennsylvania in the eighteenth and nineteenth centuries, the elk and other vital wildlife to the state's ecosystem became extinct, with many more on the way out. In response, the citizens of Pennsylvania demanded a game commission be established to help right those wrongs before it was too late.

An elk nicknamed "Scratcher" bugling in the heart of elk country. *David Anderson, 2014.*

Then the lumber industry became the vanguard of innovation and wealth creation in the state. Leaving behind barren fields of leveled forests welcomed in environmental catastrophes such as massive forest fires, devastating floods and irreversible erosion damages. From this came the Commission on Forestry, which sought to find a sustainable way to profit from the wealth of Pennsylvania's timber without endangering the wildlife or environment. Eventually, the Pennsylvania Game Commission reintroduced the elk herd and allowed for seasonal hunts but found the population struggling to survive.

By that time, coal had become king, and many unethical corporations like the Pittsburg, Shawmut and Northern Railroad Company wanted to take advantage of the unregulated market, resulting in mining towns like Force being overrun with pollution and sewage, contaminating their limited water supplies. These conditions, while barely livable for humans, proved to be another great hardship that the elk had to bear.

Enough was enough for Pennsylvanians, and Operation Scarlift sought to wash away the scars wrought by irresponsible mining practices. However, scars can never truly be purified; they will always live on in some form, serving as permanent reminders of past traumas. As such, the waterways of the Valley are still polluted, but through the many water treatment facilities, the damage from acid mine drainage is largely hidden from daily life.

The groundwork for a conservation movement had been laid by nearly two centuries of environmental abuse, which forced many to decide whether or not it was worth it to protect Pennsylvania's greatest resource: its environment. Throughout the past few decades, conservation groups like the Keystone Elk Country Alliance have made it their mission to educate the public and protect Pennsylvania's wildlife so that the mistakes of the past can be remembered yet never repeated.

In the same manner that the logging and coal industries provided economic growth for the Valley, so too does elk tourism. It has directly brought in hundreds of millions of dollars of revenue and allowed for many local businesses to flourish. Unlike its predecessors, the elk tourism industry does not pose a direct threat to the natural landscape of the area. It actively seeks the environment's revitalization and constant protection.

It took centuries to realize that in order to save the elk, and enable them to survive and thrive, Pennsylvania had to save itself first. The state needed to invest in reviving its natural wealth to as close to its original state as possible—the landscape that captivated William Penn, George Washington,

Ulysses S. Grant and Philip Tome; the same region that J.T. Rothrock, Gifford Pinchot, Charles Kalbfus and Betty Hayes fought to revitalize; and that modern environmentalists like Rawland Cogan and the Keystone Elk Country Alliance strive to protect and maintain. It was not until the state government, in partnership with conservationists, invested in the reclamation of Pennsylvania that the herd was able to thrive as it is now.

This was Pennsylvania's renaissance—the rebirth it so desperately needed.

NOTES

Introduction

1. Harrison, *History of Pennsylvania Elk Country*, 3.
2. Rawland D. Cogan (wildlife biologist and president and CEO of KECA) in discussion with the author, March 18, 2022.
3. Harrison, *History of Pennsylvania Elk Country*, 86.
4. Elk County Outfitters, https://elkcountyoutfitters.com.
5. Tome, *Pioneer Life*, 54.
6. Ibid., 43–45.
7. Ibid., 53.
8. Ibid., 75.
9. Poe, "Morning on the Wissahiccon."
10. Kosack, *Pennsylvania Game Commission*, 180.
11. Wetschler, "Deep in Elk Country."

1. Where'd All The Wild Things Go?

12. "The Last of the Wapiti: A Forty-Mile Chase After a Lone Elk. Story of the Extinction of the Race in the Great Forest of Pennsylvania," *New York Times*, October 21, 1888.
13. King, *Lore of the Last Frontier*.
14. 2018 Census Projections, U.S. Census Bureau.
15. "Last of the Wapiti."
16. "Hunting the Noble Elk: How Jack Lyman and Laroy Lyman Tracked Together," *Philadelphia Times*, June 3, 1894.
17. Keim, *Sheridan's Troopers*, 279.

18. Tome, *Pioneer Life*, 75.
19. Ibid., 55.
20. Kosack, *Pennsylvania Game Commission*, 13.
21. Abraham Beck quoted in Kosack, *Pennsylvania Game Commission*, 17.
22. Kosack, *Pennsylvania Game Commission*, 18.
23. Madson, *White-Tailed Deer*, 65–66.
24. Ibid., 50.
25. Tome, *Pioneer Life*, 21.
26. Kosack, *Pennsylvania Game Commission*, 5.
27. Ibid., 13.
28. Tome, *Pioneer Life*, 71.
29. "A Game Commission," *Lancaster Intelligencer*, January 18, 1893.
30. Dunn and Dunn, *Papers of William Penn*, 513.
31. Wessman, *History of Elk County*, 87–90.

2. Crosscut Saw

32. Dunn and Dunn, *Papers of William Penn*, 60.
33. William Penn's "Charter of Privileges," printed by Benjamin Franklin in 1701.
34. Eben, *Gottlieb Mittelberger's Journey*.
35. George Washington, October 5, 1770, in Conklin, *Report of the Department of Forestry*, 536.
36. George Washington, November 21, 1770, Conklin, *Report of the Department of Forestry*, 536.
37. Tome, *Pioneer Life*, 65.
38. Bishop in Conklin, *Report of the Department of Forestry*, 556.
39. John Lincklaen in Conklin, *Report of the Department of Forestry*, 558.
40. Conklin, *Report of the Department of Forestry*, 559.
41. Ibid., 537.
42. Conklin, *Report of the Department of Forestry*, 538.
43. Wessman, *History of Elk County*, 17.
44. Mt. Zion Historical Society, https://mtzionhistoricalsociety.org.
45. Burke, *Pioneers of Second Fork*, 81–83.
46. Ibid., 99–101.
47. Ibid., 115.
48. Ibid., 132–33.
49. Ibid., 144–45.
50. Hughes, *Lumbering in Elk County*.
51. Forrey, *History of Pennsylvania's State Parks*, 3.
52. Crocco, *History of Jay and Benezette Townships*.
53. Mary Emery in Pearsall, *History and Genealogy*, 1,258–59.
54. Crocco, *History of Jay and Benezette Townships*.
55. Ibid.
56. Tome, *Pioneer Life*, 90.

57. Ibid.
58. Ibid., 90–91.
59. Ibid., 90.
60. Horst, "Logging in the Pennsylvania," 41.
61. Pinchot, "How Conservation Began," 258.
62. New York State Forest Commission, in Pinchot, "How Conservation Began," 259.
63. "Damages from Forest Fires: They Are Much More Serious Than the Mere Financial Loss," *Philadelphia Times*, January 2, 1896.
64. Ibid.
65. Conklin, *Report of the Department of Forestry*, 553–54.
66. Swanger, "Something Akin to a Second Birth," 345–46.
67. Ibid., 347–48.
68. Taber, *Goodyears*, 553.
69. "Fierce Forest Fires: Many Houses Destroyed and Towns in Danger," *Philadelphia Inquirer*, May 19, 1896.
70. Swanger, "Something Akin to a Second Birth," 347.
71. Freedman, "Environmental Effects of Forestry."
72. Swanger, "Something Akin to a Second Birth," 346.
73. "News From All Over the State: The Damage from the Flood Not So Great as Was Expected," *Philadelphia Times*, January 9, 1895.
74. "A Field For Forestry," *Pittsburgh Dispatch*, December 17, 1891.
75. Swanger, "Something Akin to a Second Birth," 352.
76. Pinchot, "How Conservation Began," 255.
77. Swanger, "Something Akin to a Second Birth," 347.
78. Freedman, "Environmental Effects of Forestry."
79. Ibid.

3. A Mountain Man's Dream

80. "Game Commission."
81. "Harrisburg Letter: The Defeat of the Game Commission Bill," *Freeland (PA) Tribune*, April 11, 1895.
82. "Doings in Harrisburg," *Forest Republican* (Tionesta, PA), May 22, 1895.
83. Kosack, *Pennsylvania Game Commission*, 24.
84. Ibid.
85. Ibid., 25.
86. Joseph Kalbfus in Federation of Sportsmen's Clubs of Pennsylvania, *Memorial to Dr. Joseph Kalbfus*, 22.
87. Ibid., 25.
88. Joseph Kalbfus in Kosack, *Pennsylvania Game Commission*, 55.
89. Kosack, *Pennsylvania Game Commission*, 33–34.
90. Ibid., 34.
91. William T. Hornaday in Kosack, *Pennsylvania Game Commission*, 34–35.

92. "A Tragedy of the Planes," *Philadelphia Inquirer*, August 18, 1912.

93. Ibid.

94. Department of the Interior, "Shipments of Elk 1913."

95. Charles Penrose to Colonel Lloyd Brett, February 17, 1913.

96. Kosack, *Pennsylvania Game Commission*, 45.

97. Keystone Elk Country Alliance, "Elk in Pennsylvania Once More," 41–42.

98. Charles Penrose to Colonel Lloyd Brett, May 12, 1913.

99. Colonel Lloyd Brett to Charles Penrose, May 16, 1913.

100. Joseph Kalbfus in Kosack, *Pennsylvania Game Commission*, 45.

101. "Zoo/Monuments & Statues," Hershey-Derry Township Historical Society, https://hersheyhistory.pastperfectonline.com.

102. Department of the Interior, "Shipments of Elk Winter of 1914–15."

103. F.T. Arnold to the Secretary of the Interior, February 7, 1916.

104. Department of the Interior, "Shipments of Elk Winter of 1914–15."

105. F.T. Arnold to Charles Penrose, February 5, 1915.

106. F.T. Arnold to Charles Penrose, September 18, 1914.

107. Kosack, *Pennsylvania Game Commission*, 45.

108. Harrisburg Chapter Rocky Mountain Elk Foundation, "Elk Return to Pennsylvania," 1–2.

109. John Phillips in Kosack, *Pennsylvania Game Commission*, 45.

110. Kosack, *Pennsylvania Game Commission*, 50.

111. Joseph Kalbfus in Kosack, *Pennsylvania Game Commission*, 49–50.

112. Seth Gordon in Kosack, *Pennsylvania Game Commission*, 50.

113. Kosack, *Pennsylvania Game Commission*, 50.

114. Ibid.

115. Joseph Kalbfus in Kosack, *Pennsylvania Game Commission*, 48–49.

116. Kosack, *Pennsylvania Game Commission*, 49.

117. Heller, "First Elk in 1923."

118. "Buck Law Is Revived by Game Board; Limit Put on Bear Season," *Jeffersonian-Democrat*, June 16, 1932.

119. "Seasons and Bag Limits for 1932 Hunting Season," *Bradford Evening Star* and *Bradford Daily Record*, June 14, 1932.

120. Vernon Bailey in Kosack, *Pennsylvania Game Commission*, 61.

121. Ross Leffler in Kosack, *Pennsylvania Game Commission*, 62.

122. Kosack, *Pennsylvania Game Commission*, 78.

123. Ernest E. Harwood in Kosack, *Pennsylvania Game Commission*, 78.

124. Kosack, *Pennsylvania Game Commission*, 78.

125. Aldo Leopold in Kosack, *Pennsylvania Game Commission*, 81.

126. Kosack, *Pennsylvania Game Commission*, 81.

127. "Elk Wildlife Note," Pennsylvania Game Commission, https://www.pgc.pa.gov/Education/WildlifeNotesIndex/Pages/Elk.aspx.

128. Seth Gordon in Kosack, *Pennsylvania Game Commission*, 88.

4. King Coal

129. Tome, *Pioneer Life*, 65.
130. Deasy and Griess, "Geographical Significance of Recent Changes," 284.
131. Roy, *History of the Coal Miners*, 39.
132. Ibid., 42.
133. U.S. WW I Centennial Commission, https://www.worldwar1centennial.org.
134. "Father Kept Entombed Son Alive with Breath," *Daily Press*, October 23, 1936.
135. "Bootleg Miner," track 10 on Van Wagner, *North of 80*, 2002.
136. Bucktail Chapter of the National Railroad Historical Society, "Quick History of the PS&N," 12.
137. Henry Marquand & Co., "Pittsburg, Shawmut and Northern Railroad," 1.
138. Ibid.
139. Krellner, "King Coal on the Shawmut," 12–13.
140. Chiappelli, *Freight of Grapes*, 1–2.
141. Klebe, "All Aboard the Pennsy."
142. Chiappelli, *Freight of Grapes*, 1–2.
143. Krellner, "King Coal on the Shawmut," 12–13.
144. "Elk County Miners Appeal to Governor and John L. Lewis," *Kane (PA) Republican*, August 25, 1945.
145. Biederman, *Mighty Force*, 18.
146. Chiappelli, *Freight of Grapes*, 1–2.
147. Spriger, "Disease Stalks Company Village."
148. Ibid.
149. "Paralyzing Strike," *Courier-Express* (DuBois, PA), May 3, 1943.
150. Ibid.
151. Spriger, ""Disease Stalks Company Village."
152. "Elk County Miners Appeal to Governor and John L. Lewis," *Kane (PA) Republican*, August 25, 1945.
153. Biederman, *Mighty Force*, 32.
154. Ira Gabrielson in Kosack, *Pennsylvania Game Commission*, 100.
155. Kosack, *Pennsylvania Game Commission*, 104.
156. Seth Gordon in Kosack, *Pennsylvania Game Commission*, 104.
157. Albert Day in Kosack, *Pennsylvania Game Commission*, 103.
158. Clean Streams Law, section 4.
159. Leo Luttringer in Kosack, *Pennsylvania Game Commission*, 104.
160. "A Rural Slum," *Pittsburgh Post-Gazette*, August 10, 1945.
161. "Elk Wildlife Note," Pennsylvania Game Commission.
162. Pennsylvania Game Commission meeting notes in Kosack, *Pennsylvania Game Commission*, 111–12.
163. Biederman, *Mighty Force*, 81.
164. Ibid., 99.
165. Tony Coccimiglio in Biederman, *Mighty Force*, 120.
166. Fitzgerald, "Letter to the Editor."

167. Biederman, *Mighty Force*, 125.
168. "Not Always Golden," *Daily Press*, November 19, 1945.
169. Bill Davidson in Biederman, *Mighty Force*, 122.
170. Ibid.
171. "Medicine: Dr. Betty Cleans Up," *Time*, December 1945.
172. Woody Guthrie Publications Inc., https://www.woodyguthrie.org/publicationsindex.htm.

5. Operation Scarlift

173. *Constitution of the Commonwealth of Pennsylvania*, section 27.
174. Kerr, "Outdoors in Potter County."
175. Robert Broughton in Kerr. "Outdoors in Potter County."
176. Kerr, "Outdoors in Potter County."
177. "Strip Mining," Citizens Coal Council, https://www.citizenscoalcouncil.org.
178. Kosack, *Pennsylvania Game Commission*, 141–42.
179. Ibid., 148–50.
180. McConnell, Fowler and Friedrich, "Operation Scarlift," 5.
181. Logue, Stroman and Sivarajah, "Centralia Mine Fire," 21–23.
182. McConnell, Fowler and Friedrich, "Operation Scarlift," 6.
183. Ibid., 8.
184. Ibid., 22.
185. Ibid., 20.
186. Ibid., 29.
187. "Elk Wildlife Note," Philadelphia Game Commission.
188. "Brain Worm," New York State Department of Environmental Conservation, https://www.dec.ny.gov/animals/72211.html
189. Kosack, "History of Elk in Pa."
190. McConnell, Fowler and Friedrich, "Operation Scarlift," 27.
191. John Dzemyan, in Pennsylvania Game Commission, "Pennsylvania Elk," min. 18:10–18:30.
192. "Elk Wildlife Note," Pennsylvania Game Commission.
193. Cogan, "Elk Habitat Benefits Other Wildlife."
194. Kosack, *Pennsylvania Game Commission*, 180–82.
195. Rawland D. Cogan (wildlife biologist and president and CEO of KECA) in discussion with the author, March 18, 2022.
196. Lantz Hoffman in Kosack, *Pennsylvania Game Commission*, 188–89.
197. Steve Liscinsky, "How It Was: Deer Management in Pennsylvania," in *Pennsylvania Big Game Records*, edited by Bell, Maugans and Mitchell.
198. Cogan, "Elk Reproduction."
199. Kosack, *Pennsylvania Game Commission*, 201.
200. "How We Conserve: Protect. Support. Enhance. Open," Rocky Mountain Elk Foundation, https://www.rmef.org.
201. Kosack, *Pennsylvania Game Commission*, 207.

202. Bower, "Outdoor Diary."
203. "'Elk Patrol' Keeps Spectators in Line," *Indiana (PA) Gazette*, August 16, 2002.
204. Ibid.
205. Knapp, "Three-Year Plan Aims."
206. Cogan, "Elk Habitat Benefits," 2001.
207. Ibid.
208. Cavazza, "Restoring the Bennett Branch," 7.
209. Ibid., 11.
210. Ibid., 16–17.
211. Mulhollem, "Trout River Reborn."
212. Cogan, discussion.
213. Harrisburg Chapter Rocky Mountain Elk Foundation, "Elk Return to Pennsylvania," 1–2.

6. A New Song for an Old Forest

214. Moyer, "Governor's Outdoor Task Force," 5.
215. Moyer, "Elk Country Visitor Center."
216. Ibid.
217. "Our Green Building," Elk Country Visitor Center Website, https://elkcountryvisitorcenter.com.
218. Pennsylvania Department of Conservation and Natural Resources, "Sinnemahoning State Park," https://www.dcnr.pa.gov/StateParks/FindAPark/SinnemahoningStatePark/Pages/default.aspx.
219. Pennsylvania Department of Conservation and Natural Resources, "Kinzua Bridge State Park," https://www.dcnr.pa.gov/StateParks/FindAPark/KinzuaBridgeStatePark/Pages/default.aspx.
220. Cogan, discussion.
221. Ibid.
222. Ibid.
223. Ibid.
224. Ibid.
225. Ibid.
226. Ibid.
227. Ibid.
228. Ibid.
229. Ibid.
230. Ibid.
231. Ibid.
232. Ibid.
233. Ibid.
234. Ibid.
235. Ibid.

BIBLIOGRAPHY

Arnold, F.T. F.T. Arnold to Charles Penrose. Fort Yellowstone, WY. September 18, 1914. KECA Private Collection.
———. F.T. Arnold to Charles Penrose. Fort Yellowstone, WY. October 24, 1914.
———. F.T. Arnold to Charles Penrose. Fort Yellowstone, WY. February 5, 1915.
———. F.T. Arnold to the Secretary of the Interior. Fort Yellowstone, WY. February 7, 1916.
Bell, Bob, Betsy Maugans and Bob Mitchell, eds. *Pennsylvania Big Game Records 1965–1986*. Harrisburg: Pennsylvania Game Commission, 1988.
Biederman, Marcia. *A Mighty Force: Dr. Elizabeth Hayes and Her War for Public Health*. Guilford, CT: Prometheus Books, 2021.
Boone, Joel T. *A Medical Survey of the Bituminous-Coal Industry*. Washington, D.C.: U.S. Department of the Interior Coal Mines Administration, 1947.
Bower, Wes. "Outdoor Diary." *Daily News* (Huntingdon, PA), September 5, 1995.
Brett, Lloyd. Colonel Brett Lloyd to Charles Penrose, Fort Yellowstone, WY. May 16, 1913.
Bucktail Chapter of the National Railroad Historical Society. "A Quick History of the PS&N." *Daily Press* (St. Marys, PA), April 3, 1997.
Burke, James. *Pioneers of Second Fork*. Weedville, PA: Mt. Zion Historical Society, 2009.
Cavazza, Eric E. *Reclaiming Abandoned Mine Lands Reduces Impact of Acid Mine Drainage in the Bennett Branch Basin*. Washington, DC: U.S. Environmental Protection Agency, Office of Water, 2016.
———. "Restoring the Bennett Branch Sinnemahoning Creek, Clearfield and Elk Counties, Pennsylvania." Paper presented at the National Meeting of the American Society of Mining and Reclamation, Pittsburgh, PA, 2010.
Chiappelli, Donald F. *Freight of Grapes and Memories of Hoodlebugs*. Bennetts Valley Senior Center, 2016.

Clean Streams Law. June 22, 1937. https://pennstatelaw.psu.edu/_file/aglaw/
  Marcellus_Shale/Clean_Streams_Law_Update.pdf.

Cogan, Rawland D. "Elk Habitat Benefits Other Wildlife, Too." *Pennsylvania Game
  News*, August 2001.

———. "Elk Reproduction." *Pennsylvania Game News*, September 1998.

Cogan, Rawland D., Robert Cordes and Jon DeBerti. "Pennsylvania's Elk Trap
  and Transfer Project." *Pennsylvania Game News*, May 2001.

Conklin, Robert S. *Report of the Department of Forestry of the State of Pennsylvania for the
  Years 1912–1913*. Harrisburg: Pennsylvania Department of Forestry, 1913.

Constitution of the Commonwealth of Pennsylvania. Harrisburg, PA, 1873. https://www.
  legis.state.pa.us/WU01/LI/LI/CT/HTM/00/00.HTM.

Crocco, S.R. *History of Jay and Benezette Townships in Bennett's Valley*. Benezette, PA:
  Bennett's Valley News, 1966.

Deasy, George F., and Phyllis R Griess. "Geographical Significance of Recent
  Changes in Mining in the Bituminous Coal Fields of Pennsylvania." *Economic
  Geography* 33, no. 4 (October 1957): 283–98.

Defebaugh, James Elliott. *History of the Lumber Industry of America*. Vol. 2. Chicago:
  American Lumberman, 1907.

Department of the Interior. "Shipments of Elk 1913." Yellowstone National Park,
  Office of Superintendent. Yellowstone Park, WY, 1913.

———. "Shipments of Elk Winter of 1914–1915." Yellowstone National Park,
  Office of Superintendent. Yellowstone Park, WY, February 7, 1916.

Dunn, Richard S., and Mary Maples Dunn. *The Papers of William Penn*. Vol 2.
  Philadelphia: University of Pennsylvania Press, 1982.

Eben, Carl Theodore, trans. *Gottlieb Mittelberger's Journey to Pennsylvania in the Year
  1750*. Philadelphia: J.J. McVey, 1898.

The Federation of Sportsmen's Clubs of Pennsylvania. *The Memorial to Dr. Joseph
  Kalbfus*. Pennsylvania State University Library, July 1940.

Fitzgerald, John F. "Letter to the Editor." *Pittsburgh Post-Gazette*, November 23, 1945.

Forrey, William C. *History of Pennsylvania's State Parks*. Harrisburg, PA: Bureau of
  State Parks, Office of Resources Management, Department of Environmental
  Resources, 1984.

Freedman, Bill. "Environmental Effects of Forestry." In *Environmental Science*.
  Halifax, NS: Dalhousie University Libraries, 2018.

Harrisburg Chapter Rocky Mountain Elk Foundation. "Elk Return to
  Pennsylvania: 100th Anniversary of Reintroduction 1913–2013." *Old Post*,
  February 2, 2013.

Harrison, Ralph. *The History of Pennsylvania Elk Country*. Mechanicsburg:
  Pennsylvania Forestry Association, 2008.

Heller, Clinton. "First Elk in 1923." *Pennsylvania Game News*, October 1969.

Henry Marquand & Co. "The Pittsburg, Shawmut and Northern Railroad
  Preliminary Offering." New York City, August 1899.

Horst, Mel. *Logging in the Pennsylvania North Woods*. Lebanon, PA: Applied Arts
  Publishers, 1971.

Hughes, Helen. *Lumbering in Elk County*. Ridgway, PA: Elk County Historical Society, 2002.

Keim, De B. Randolph. *Sheridan's Troopers on the Border*. N.p.: Digital Scanning, Incorporated, 1999.

Kerr, Del. "Outdoors in Potter County." *Potter Enterprise* (Wellsboro, PA), April 28, 1971.

Keystone Elk Country Alliance. "Elk in Pennsylvania Once More: Howard Eaton Breaks All Records for Successful Transportation of Animals Released in Two State Reserves." *In the Open*, February 1913.

King, Samuel A. *Lore of the Last Frontier in Pennsylvania*. Map published by the Clearfield County Historical Society. Dubois, PA. 1960.

Klebe, Alexandra. "All Aboard the Pennsy." Penn State University Libraries, https://pabook.libraries.psu.edu.

Knapp, Jeff. "Three-Year Plan Aims to Spread Habitat of State's Elk." *Indiana (PA) Gazette*, October 5, 1997.

Kosack, Joe. "History of Elk in Pa." Pennsylvania Game Commission, https://www.pgc.pa.gov.

———. *The Pennsylvania Game Commission 1895–1995: 100 Years of Wildlife Conservation*. Harrisburg: Pennsylvania Game Commission, 1995.

Krellner, Bill. "King Coal on the Shawmut." *Daily Press*. March 29, 2001. St. Marys, PA.

Logue, James, Robert Stroman and Kandiah Sivarajah. "The Centralia Mine Fire: An Overview of Community Health Surveillance Efforts." *Journal of Environmental Health* 54, no. 1 (July/August 1991): 21–23.

Madson, John. *The White-Tailed Deer*. East Alton, IL: Winchester Western Division Olin Mathieson Chemical Corporation Conservation Department, 1961.

McConnell, C.H., Donald E. Fowler and Andrew E. Friedrich. "Operation Scarlift—Mine Drainage Abatement." Paper presented at the American Society of Civil Engineers, Philadelphia, PA, September 27–October 1, 1976.

"A Medical Survey of the Bituminous-Coal Industry." *Monthly Labor Review* 64, no. 6 (1947): 997–1002.

Moyer, Ben. "Elk Country Visitors Center to Boost Tourism." *Pittsburgh Post-Gazette*, April 8, 2007.

———. "Governor's Outdoor Task Force Report." Department of Conservation and Natural Resources. Harrisburg, PA. 2008.

Mulhollem, Jeff. "Trout River Reborn in the PA Wilds." *Outdoor News*, September 27, 2012.

Pearsall, Clarence. *History and Genealogy of the Pearsall Family in England and America*. San Francisco, CA: H.S. Crocker Company, 1928.

Penn, William. "The Charter of Privileges." Philadelphia: Published by Benjamin Franklin, 1701.

Pennsylvania Department of Environmental Protection. "Bennett Branch Sinnemahoning Creek Watershed TMDL: Cameron, Clearfield and Elk Counties." § (2008).

————. "Hollywood AMD Treatment Plant Abandoned Mine Reclamation Project." Contract No. AMD 17(1416)202.1 DGS 193-37. 2013

Pennsylvania Game Commission. "Pennsylvania Elk: Celebrating 100 Years—Long Version." YouTube. March 3, 2014.

Penrose, Charles. Charles Penrose to Colonel Lloyd Brett, Harrisburg, PA, February 17, 1913.

————. Charles Penrose to Colonel Lloyd Brett, Philadelphia, PA, May 12, 1913.

Pinchot, Gifford. "How Conservation Began in the United States." *Agricultural History Society* 11, no. 4 (October 1937).

Poe, Edgar Allan. "Morning on the Wissahiccon." In *The Opal: A Pure Gift for the Holy Days*. New York: J.C. Riker, 1844.

Rothrock, J.T. "On the Growth of the Forestry Idea in Pennsylvania." *Proceedings of the American Philosophical Society* 32 (1894): 333.

Roy, Andrew. *A History of the Coal Miners of the United States*. Columbus, OH: I.L. Trauger Printing Company, 1903.

Spriger, Ray. "Company Financing Smells of Slums." *Pittsburgh Post-Gazette*, August 18, 1945.

————. "Disease Stalks Company Village." *Pittsburgh Post-Gazette*, August 17, 1945.

Swanger, Rebecca D. "Something Akin to a Second Birth: Joseph Trimble Rothrock and the Formation of the Forestry Movement in Pennsylvania, 1839–1922." *Pennsylvania Magazine of History and Biography* 134, no. 4 (October 2010).

Taber, Thomas, III. *The Goodyears: An Empire in the Hemlocks*. Williamsport, PA: Lycoming Printing Company, 1971.

Tome, Phillip. *Pioneer Life, or 30 Years a Hunter*. N.p., 1854.

Wessman, Alice L. *A History of Elk County, Pennsylvania 1981*. Ridgway, PA: Elk County Historical Society. 1991.

Wetschler, Ed. "Deep in Elk Country, Pennsylvania." *New York Times*, October 7, 2005.

ABOUT THE AUTHOR

Mario Chiappelli is a native of Weedville, Pennsylvania, right in the heart of Elk Country. His family has lived in the Bennetts Valley area since his great-great-grandparents immigrated there from Italy in the early twentieth century. Most of his ancestors worked in the neighboring coal mines, and from them, the values of hard work, community involvement and the need to provide for your family at all costs were instilled in him.

Since he was two years old, Mario has been involved with Pennsylvania's elk. His grandfather Donald and uncle Robbie run and operate an elk hunt guiding service, and during the first reintroduced hunt in 2002, Mario was there all week with his father, Bryan. Elk have always been a significant part of his life.

Some of Mario's earliest memories are hunting deer, squirrel and turkey on his family's land in Rock Hill, in between Caledonia and Medix Run, and fishing the streams of First Fork in Sinnemahoning, Wycoff and Wharton. Pennsylvania's environment has shaped his outlook on the world from a young age. The streams throughout his home were polluted with acid mine drainage and left unfishable until the completion of the Hollywood AMD Treatment Plant in 2013. This facility, and its positive effects, showed Mario early on that many environmental and ecological mistakes were made, but even the most disastrous were capable of being fixed.

In May 2022, Mario graduated from Bucknell University in Lewisburg, Pennsylvania, with degrees in computer engineering and history. An unlikely combo of academic interests. It was not until his junior year that he decided to pursue a second major in the field of history. Mario's fascination with the subject stemmed from his early childhood, when he would watch the History Channel with his grandparents Emmanuel and Janet Pretti. Since then, he has enjoyed learning and studying history, no matter the subject.

The push to pursue the degree at Bucknell came from his first history professor, Claire Campbell, who believed that Mario's passion for history and strong work ethic would make it possible to accomplish. In order to earn the degree, Mario had to take summer classes and remove all future elective space. Additionally, he needed to craft a thirty-page analytical history report on the subject of his choosing. Originally titled "The Rebirth of Pennsylvania's Elk Country," a previous, and significantly shorter, version of this book was submitted as that assignment. Then, over the following two years, that original work was reshaped and expanded into *Preserving the Pennsylvania Wilds*.

Mario currently lives in State College, Pennsylvania, where he works as a software engineer, but he still visits the Pennsylvania Wilds, his home, whenever he can.